**May Sarton** is an internationally acclaimed poet and novelist. Her much-loved series of autobiographical works include *Journal of a Solitude* (The Women's Press, 1985), which reflects upon the inner life of the creative writer, as well as *After the Stroke* (The Women's Press, 1988), where the author chronicles her fight back to health after suffering a stroke. *Endgame* (The Women's Press, 1992) saw her once again struggling with illness, but overcoming all obstacles to continue her writing; and *Encore* (1993) marked her triumphant return to full health, in her eightieth year.

The Women's Press also publish May Sarton's novels: *As We Are Now* (1983), the story of one woman's spirited fight for dignity in a home for the elderly; *A Reckoning* (1984), about a woman's reconciliation with her own life as she faces death; *The Magnificent Spinster* (1986), celebrating the freedom and courage of two spinsters; *The Education of Harriet Hatfield* (1990), a courageous novel of a lesbian struggling against ignorance and prejudice; and her classic early novel, *Mrs Stevens Hears the Mermaids Singing* (1993). Her specially selected volume of poetry, *Halfway to Silence*, was published by The Women's Press in 1993.

May Sarton was born in Europe, but for most of her life has made the East Coast of America her home.

**Also by May Sarton from The Women's Press:**

**Fiction**
*As We Are Now* (1983)
*A Reckoning* (1984)
*The Magnificent Spinster* (1986)
*The Education of Harriet Hatfield* (1990)
*Mrs Stevens Hears the Mermaids Singing* (1993)

**Autobiography**
*Journal of a Solitude* (1985)
*After the Stroke* (1988)
*Endgame* (1993)
*Encore: A Journal of the Eightieth Year* (1993)

**Poetry**
*Halfway to Silence* (1993)

# May Sarton

# I KNEW A PHOENIX

*Sketches for an Autobiography*

*To*

*Anne Longfellow Thorp*

*and*

*Céline Dangotte Limbosch*

Published in Great Britain by The Women's Press Ltd, 1995
A member of the Namara Group
34 Great Sutton Street, London EC1V 0DX

First published in the United States of America by
W W Norton & Company, Inc, 1969

The articles, 'In My Father's House', 'Wondelgem: The House in the Country',
'O My America!', 'I Knew a Phoenix in My Youth', 'A Wild Green Place', and
'A Belgian School' (under the title 'Titi') originally appeared, in somewhat
different form, in *The New Yorker*. 'That Winter in Paris' originally appeared
as 'Goodbye to a World' in *The Reporter*.

Grateful acknowledgement is made to Eva Le Galliene and Leonard Woolf for
permission to quote from their letters; and to Dr P Sidney de Q Cabot and
Richard Boyle O'Reilly Hocking, Trustees of the late Richard Cabot's papers, for
permission to reprint a letter from Dr Richard Cabot; to Harcourt, Brace and
Company, Inc, for permission to reprint six lines from 'The Good Servant' from
*Ceremony And Other Poems*, copyright, 1950, by Richard Wilbur; to Alfred A
Knopf Incorporated, for permission to quote briefly from *The Letters of
Katherine Mansfield*; and to Houghton Mifflin Company, for permission to
reprint 'Peace' from *The Complete Poetical Works of Edward Roland Sill* (1906).

British Library Cataloguing-in-Publication Data
Sarton, May
 I Knew a Phoenix: Sketches for an
 Autobiography. - New ed
 I. Title
 813.52

ISBN 0 7043 4392 4

Printed and bound in Great Britain by
Cox & Wyman Ltd, Reading, Berks

# Contents

*May Sarton and her father George Sarton*
*– photograph by her mother, 1929.*

# I

## *The Fervent World*

"I knew a phoenix in my youth, so let
them have their day."

W. B. YEATS

*"In my father's house..."*

## "In My Father's House"

"In my father's house——," my father used to begin, wreathed in an enormous smile. As he grew older, after my mother's death, his memories of this rather somber house opposite the church of St. Michel in Ghent, took on a rich patina. Sitting opposite him in his house in Cambridge, Massachusetts, for our ritualistic Sunday dinner, I savored the short pause while some shadowy glory took on substance in his mind. I could hear the sound of herbs being chopped for the soup in that faraway kitchen, for in my grandfather's house this was the sure sign that dinner was about to be served. I could see the long table set for a dinner of twelve, the hard rolls wrapped in damask turbans at each place, the rows of wineglasses, including *flûtes* for champagne at dessert. (Of this glittering army, one survived the '14-'18 war, a green glass on a crystal stem). My father and I poured ourselves another glass of American Pinot, but our palates were far away, soothed by the glowing sequence of Chablis, Burgundies, Sauternes and Champagnes poured by my grandfather with proper solemnity, and honored, no doubt, with a long and flowery

[ *11* ]

toast by Oncle Adolphe, the literary member of the family, who taught French literature in a Lycée in Brussels, and was convinced that anything written since Chateaubriand had better be passed over in silence. "In my father's house," my father used to remind me, "at formal dinners we allowed two bottles per male guest and one per female guest."

Certain moments, certain foods introduced the magical phrase—meat loaf was one. It raised without fail the ghost of that ineffable *pain de veau* which haunted my father's American cook as an old mistress may haunt a wife. However much care she had put into the seasoning, however delicately browned and firm the meat loaf might be, its appearance on the table was always followed by a nostalgic reference to "my father's house" and to that soupçon of sage—was it sage?—that made all the difference. What could the present do against that savory past?

The frame of these memories was as bourgeois as a Balzac novel, from the yearly calls of the wine merchants (Germans who dealt in French wines, which the customer bought by the barrel and bottled himself), those solemn and prolonged negotiations, to the rolls of fine linen stored in the attic, to the enormous dinners—fourteen courses lasting late into the night. But within the frame, life was rich and eccentric. This was perhaps partly due to circumstances, to the fact that the house was inhabited only by an old man (was my grandfather ever young?) and his only son, George Sarton. Alfred Sarton, my grandfather, was a confirmed bachelor, who had for a brief interlude happened to be married, or so, at least, he appeared to me, as the little phrase brought

[ *12* ]

him into focus (ultra-sensitive, sardonic, with bright deep-set eyes) before he disappeared again into the dark house where only the dining table shone in a bright light.

What of the mysterious young woman who moved so briefly in and out of that house, who died of a hemorrhage a year after George's birth because she was too modest to call for help, while her husband, swinging his cane, ready to go out, waited for her in vain? Here the little phrase does not help. Here all is in shadow, except for the large photograph in an oval gold frame that always hung over my father's bed, the photograph of a dark, not pretty, but charming woman in an elegant riding habit, the long ostrich plume in her hat curling round her neck, and a small crop in one hand. Of her we know almost nothing: that she shocked her husband's family by buying her gloves by the dozen, that she loved candied violets and drank *fleur d'oranger*, that she played Chopin. Innocent and extravagant she was—and perhaps lonely, for she had been brought up by her Uncle Hippolyte Van Sieleghem, a notary in Bruges, a man of high principles and no sense of humor, whose idea of child education was to spread a table with candies and then make the children put them all away without tasting one; and she left Bruges to marry a man twenty years older than herself. She had the rich musical temperament of her family, the Van Halmés, set a key higher than the rather somber Sartons. *"Vive le désordre,"* she wrote her adored brother Carlos. "Your necktie has been unearthed in a corner of the house." When she was twenty-four and expecting her first child, Carlos came to Ghent for a visit. "The cradle had arrived the night before," he writes in his Journal, "and they showed it to me. It couldn't be more *coquet*. Frankly, I find it charming. The inside is lined with blue satin; the outer edge is ornamented with lace and ribbons. The cradle itself is walnut. It represents a basket resting on two elegant feet, one of which rises above it to about five feet in height and supports a huge cream-coloured curtain lined in blue silk. The child has not arrived but everything has been foreseen including the manner in which it will be brought up. Léonie intends to bring him or her up in the English fashion, which is to say without swaddling clothes or bonnet. From the very first day the child will wear a long dress." And four months later Carlos confides to his journal: "Alfred and Léonie are delightful to see. They are so happy to have a baby that one wants to have one oneself at once." This is the only note of happiness to be found among the family papers to do with my grandfather Sarton, for a year later Léonie was dead. And all around her hangs the perfume of sadness, the silence her husband never broke to tell little George something of that vanished young mother who so soon became younger than her son. Her charm, her little ways, her smile, the tenderness for which the boy starved, were locked up with the piano, and never opened again.

Instead George was pampered and neglected by the maids. If he was ill, they kindly took his medicine for him, especially if it had a nasty taste, but, ignorant and irresponsible, they were about as far from an English Nanny as can be imagined. Loneliness haunted his memories of babyhood, but it was an active imaginative loneliness, not without a streak of Flemish humor. When he was still eating in a high chair, George was allowed to be present at dinner, but if he so much as babbled a single word, his father, without raising his head from his newspaper, reached forward to touch the bell (a round brass bell on a stand, tapped with one finger) and when the maid appeared, said simply, *"Enlevez-le."* When George was alone at a meal, formally served him in the dining room in his high chair, and he did not like something he was given to eat, he repeated the lordly gesture and the lordly phrase and was delighted to see that, like "Open Sesame" in reverse, he could thus have the unhappy cabbage, or whatever it was, removed from sight.

His grammar school, too, was filled with chances for dramatic action. One teacher so often came to class in a highly inebriated state that the field for practical jokes was wide open. George trained the students to disappear under their desks at a given signal, while the bewildered master who had been fumbling at the door, entered a silent and apparently empty classroom. Hardly had he adjusted himself to this phenomenon, when, at another signal, the entire class popped into view. Was it this master who, at the end of his patience, relegated George to the back bench alone? And then, while the boy pretended to smoke a pipe in sublime indifference, suddenly shouted, *"Sarton, tu pues la paresse jusqu'ici!"* ("I can smell your laziness from here!") And is this why my father, great scholar though he was, always had a special tender feeling for the weak student, the ugly duckling? For so many years he must have seemed one himself, a little boy whose new clothes were bought two sizes too big for him so they would last longer. This may have worked pretty well when the clothes were too large, but especially in the case of shoes, it made the third year of

[ 15 ]

their wearing an agony. He was then further isolated by his clumsiness in a coat too long and shoes, perhaps, too small; thrown more and more inward, or into that love of practical jokes which is, perhaps, always the desperate attempt of the solitary and the shy to communicate.

Still, there were compensations. It was surely a grand sight to see one's father dressed in his Civil Service uniform as Engineer in Chief to the State Railroads, a uniform that looked rather like that of an admiral in a Gilbert and Sullivan Opera, heavy with gold braid and accompanied by a cocked hat with a plume. I can remember my awe as a child, finding in the attic a box of his decorations, including a sunburst from a Persian potentate who must have rated a very grand special train. When my father was at boarding school in Chimay, he sauntered down to the station one fine morning and ostentatiously let it be known that he was waiting for the eleven o'clock from Brussels.

"There is no train at this hour, young man," the station guard told him in the self-important tone dear to minor civil servants.

"Wait and see," the young man answered, and, sure enough, at precisely eleven his father rode in on a special train. I feel that this triumph, this shared family joke against the bureaucracy was typical of the Sartons, and that my father's relationship with his father, in many ways helplessly impersonal, found its moments of intimacy on just such occasions, and their deep-set eyes, so alike in their mischief and melancholy, twinkled at each other then in perfect understanding, as father and son went off to have an apéritif.

The high-spirited little boy was turning into a young

[ *16* ]

man full of intellectual curiosity and innocent arrogance. In his last two years at Chimay he not only devised a system by which, on the nights when the school was given mussels (a great delicacy) for supper, the younger boys had to serve themselves first, a meal composed chiefly of empty shells and juice, but he also wrote a four-act drama in German and conceived the idea that Greek was the only ancient language worth bothering with, but that he must also be given lessons in Sanskrit. The Director of the Athénée took umbrage and George received a series of characteristically amused, tender letters from his aunts and uncles, suggesting that he hold his horses. The tone of these is best conveyed by a letter from his bachelor Oncle Arthur when, a year later, young George suddenly decided that the University was simply an impediment to his own studies. "*Belle affaire!*" Oncle Arthur wrote, and one sees the smile hiding itself behind his black mustache. "University studies would be simply a waste of time, of that precious time you owe to philosophy, and your relations with the civilized world. I'm afraid, for my part, that you have been led to feel this profound disgust for universities in general and professors in particular because each and several, far from weaving you laurel crowns and leading you in triumph to the Capital, have the unfortunate pretension to cling somewhat to their own ideas, to their own persons, that is to say their authority, in refusing to consecrate an adolescent king."

My father, when we had embarked on a third glass of wine, liked to refer to himself as an impertinent young man. And often cited as an example his friendship, when he was still at Chimay, a boy of sixteen in fact, with an old Count, a member of the aristocracy of Ghent, who was a well-known *bon vivant,* and enjoyed the young man's company over an apéritif. Expanding on life in general on one of these occasions, the old Count asked George what he thought of the idea of fasting one day a week. The young man's eyes must have twinkled behind his glasses very much as his own father's did, as he suggested that he himself would advise going on a humdinger of a binge one day a week and fasting for the other six. "I did not see him much after that," the story ended, but the ripples of my father's beaming smile seemed to go on and on.

Once in a while, on rare and festive occasions, perhaps over a glass of sparkling burgundy at Christmas, my father went back a generation and spoke of his grandmother's house. His grandmother came from France (her name had been de Schodt) and brought with her, perhaps, a grace of heart lacking among the Flemings. At any rate those memories were always, it seemed, like a burst of sunlight, as if there at his grandmother's the boy had known something of tenderness and warmth. She looked rather like Queen Victoria, placid and maternal, and was followed to Mass (so my father often told me) by her fourteen cats. The cats waited quietly at the door and after Mass accompanied her home again, their tails in air. At his grandmother's there was escape from the long Sunday dinner to the garden at the back, to the Victorian grotto at the end, which may have been ornamental, but was also useful, at least to the cats who managed to steal—on one occasion—a partridge and, pursued by the Flemish cook, chased each other around the Gothic protuberances like some grotesque vision by Hieronymus Bosch.

It is clear why this house was always spoken of as "my grandmother's house" and not that of her husband, Séverin Bonaventure Sarton of the glorious name, but the somewhat inglorious character. He was a *Receveur de Contributions*, collector of city taxes, and conducted his business in a small front room in his own house. If more than three people accumulated in the waiting room, he lost his head completely and rushed back to his wife, wringing his hands, and crying out, "What am I to do with all these people?" Then Agnès Thérèse answered calmly, "Just take them one at a time, dear. It will be all right," and went on turning the pears ripening on cotton wool in a drawer in the dining room. And, meek as a lamb, soothed by this sight of order in chaos, her husband returned to face the terrifying "crowd."

This timid soul and his indomitable wife produced the Sarton clan, Alfred and that formidable row of boys who grew up to be my father's uncles, Arthur, Adolphe, Ernest, Jules, and the two older daughters, Hélène and Elisa. Adolphe, the golden-tongued professor of literature, we have met. Jules, a retired army captain, lived in Antwerp and exhausted his small nephew by taking him on interminable walks to see the port, bearing down hard on the superiority of Antwerp to that backwater, Ghent. A quarter of a century later he loomed before me as the type of authoritarian; I hated to be forced to kiss his prickly red beard, and the atmosphere of his house, somber, filled with the reverberations of his fierce temper, made me extremely grateful that we did not live in Belgium. Probably he was afraid of women, and so, bullied them. He only emerged for me as a human being, the other day, when I found an old letter of his to his nephew and caught at last the flavor of this irascible man. "Yes, my dear George, I summoned all the Sartons, who have never been political chameleons (style of my regretted father) nor mere donkey hack-writers (always the same style for which I have the greatest respect) to take my stand not with the young but with the old dogs of whom we are. I am a liberal, because I'm the enemy of pundits and dogmas, because I am independent, because I don't want to be led either by donkeys or foxes, because I am practical. I believe we must make as many people happy as possible here on earth, that we must lift the moral level of the workingman and not enslave or exploit him to satisfy our ambition: Less talk, my dear nephew, more acts!"

Ernest, on the other hand, was the black sheep, a country doctor who gambled and whose debts were always being paid by one member of the family after another. Arthur followed in his father's footsteps in the civil service and remained a bachelor, fond of giving advice, warm-hearted, sharing his nephew's love of Greek. Poor Hélène, muffled perhaps by her aggressive brothers, declined into permanent spinsterhood. She is evoked rather cruelly by Carlos Van Halmé in the same journal where he records his dazzled contemplation of George's cradle: "I have on my left Mademoiselle Hélène Sarton of a very respectable age and who has retained of girlhood only the name. We talk of everything—politics, philosophy, everything under the sun: she is very powerful, my neighbor, but desperately thin. We end by approaching the Chapter of Marriage. 'Don't you think,' says Mademoiselle Hélène, 'that a house without women is awfully sad; I understand that a woman may live alone, but a man must marry.' I answer, 'Mademoiselle, I share your views, a house without a

woman is—an oyster shell without a pearl inside it.'"
Hélène ended her days as a boarder in a convent where
she assiduously studied the market and amassed a small
fortune, which she kept in a trunk, in a constant state of
alarm lest the nuns steal it. I remember her, very old,
terrifying to a child, for she seemed so dried up that her
desperate efforts to weep did not succeed in squeezing
out a single tear, and after my visits there, I felt ill with
pity and horror. So it was with the strange sense that a
door was opening into a closed world that I found one of
her last letters to that beloved nephew far away in
America, and the breath of poetry touched my cheek like
a blush. "What joins me to *you* whom I love so much, are
the clouds, the same ones that we contemplate. You
have time in the evening to see them, I hope, since you
see your cat on the roof, and that makes me think of
your father who made a cat jump after a spool. They are
loved in this establishment and I caress them when I
have the occasion to do so. They have always been one
of my passions."

Curiously enough, Elisa, the oldest of the family,
was the one real cosmopolitan, for she became, as Mère
Marie d'Agréda, a member of the Société de Marie-
Réparatrice, and finally Mother Superior, and lived within the Order at various times in Seville, Strasbourg, and
Mauritius. In the one photograph we have of this remarkable woman in her blue habit, the face, framed in
stiff white, looks down the years with a wonderful
warmth and practical goodness. What a generous mouth,
as well as the dark deep-set eyes that were a family
characteristic! There is nothing austere about it; it is a
real Flemish face, broad, humorous, compassionate. I
was not surprised to find how her goodness found expres-

sion even at the end, when on the day of her death, as it happened that the convent where she had retired was celebrating the twenty-fifth anniversary of one of its members, she tried to keep herself alive till evening; nor that late that night, though she had been in fearful pain, she whispered to the sisters around her, "How long it is, isn't it?—especially for you!"

Elisa's history is the more remarkable in that her brothers were ardent liberals, and in Flemish Belgium, this means almost inevitably anticlerical. My grandfather, Alfred Sarton, was himself a Mason and felt so strongly about religious matters that he made a separate will giving his brothers authority to "keep at a distance and if necessary to separate from my person, at all times and in all places, all priests of any creed and any other persons whose religious obsessions they might fear in regard to me. They will take all measures they judge necessary, and if need be will have recourse to public authority." The obituaries all mention "the firmness of his anticlerical opinions" and legend has it that when he died (well protected by his brothers, it would seem!) there were so many carriages at the funeral that the faithful could not get to Mass at St. Michel, the church opposite his house. This, it seems, was his last little joke. But he was liberal enough to allow his son freedom of choice in these matters, or perhaps he gave in to the wishes of his mother, the formidable lady of the cats, in regard to her grandson's education. At any rate, little George was given religious instruction on condition that he could make up his own mind when the time came for his First Communion.

George, at nine, decided to withdraw. This was the

first of many independent decisions the boy made as he came into himself, some of them wilful, some of them wise, and all of them together giving him the reputation of being an eccentric by the time he was twenty. The most shocking of these, worse even than his vegetarianism, or his socialism, must have been the auction of his father's famous wine cellar after Alfred Sarton's death—and the most important was surely his determination to write a history of science. But the first made it possible for my parents to buy the lovely house in the country near Ghent, where I was born, and the second changed in forty years from a preposterous dream to the monumental *Introduction to the History of Science,* which is such a fertile reality to scholars today.

When people who still remember young George Sarton speak of him, they always smile. They always sigh, "*Ah, ce Georges!*" and tell one or another of the stories that are growing into a legend. For instance, when he was tired of studying, he would go down to the station with a Baedeker, pretend to be a tourist, and ask a cabby to "show him the town." Perhaps he might even persuade the cabby, as a special favor, to initiate him into that tiny shop in a cellar where, since time immemorial, two glass jars on the single counter have contained the only wares—two kinds of *boules,* one dark, one light, hard candy, which, for the true Gantois, are as evocative as the hoot of a canalboat about to make a turn, or as Proust's *madeleine* was to him. Ghent is an endlessly fascinating city, small enough so that a boy could know its every alley, but big enough to boast an opera of its own and a university; beautiful—a city where merchant princes built their great houses in every decade from the fifteenth century down through the nineteenth; and as mysterious as Bruges but more alive, since its canals are still in use as thoroughfares for the barges of coal, wheat and flax. To George Sarton the city opened the passionate hours of discovery in secondhand book-stores; the journeys down the Lys, a volume of poems in one's pocket, to eat the first asparagus with hard-boiled eggs and beer at a café on the waterside; and always, every hour, the churchbells ringing, so that a small boy lost in Jules Verne or a young man discovering Nietzsche, Maurice Maeterlinck, or Verhaeren would lift his head, startled at the passage of time. There were the cafés where a habitué kept his clay pipe with his name written on it. During one year of great fatigue, George had pipes all over the city, like a clubman with many clubs. Here he wandered, smoking and composing the early romantic books he wrote under the pseudonym of Dominique de Bray, when he thought he would be a poet, and with no idea yet that he would soon be getting a doctorate in celestial mechanics, then leave Belgium forever as a refugee in the 1914–18 war, and eventually become the first American professor of a new discipline called the History of Science—nor, for that matter, that the poet in him would take root and reappear in his daughter, a gen-eration later.

The days when my father and I drank American Pinot, and he evoked the past for me, are over, but the little phrase still hangs in the air, as all the loneliness and struggle and the rich life of the somber old house and the city in which it stood are distilled in the aroma of the Lenten lobster, or that ineffable *pain de veau,* "in my father's house."

*"Now, thinking of my mother, I think of the little girl in Wales who learned so much through such unconventional means."*

## A Wild Green Place

"Tell me about Wales. Tell me what it was like," I used to beg my mother when I was a child. I never tired of hearing her descriptions of the wild green place, hearing those bits and pieces of a story that I did not come to know in its entirety until several years after her death. Then I found out what "it was like"—what it was really like, the whole story written down in her own hand and left among her papers for someone (or no one) to find, not a tale told to a little daughter but the pinning down once and for all of a complex experience that had haunted her. It has been like putting one of those tightly curled Japanese flowers into a glass of water and watching it open, for this early memory of my mother's seems to reveal in essence the flowering of a lifetime.

My mother belonged to the Elwes family, of Suffolk, England. Gervase Elwes, her father, was a civil engineer and responsible for laying out railways, roads and bridges in India, Spain and Canada, and therefore he was often away from home for long periods of time. I have gathered that my grandmother loved him almost to the exclusion of her two children, Hugh and Mabel. It apparently never occurred to her, when she and her husband set out for Canada (where Gervase Elwes had a job working on the extension of the Winnipeg waterworks), that it might seem strange to abandon these two—nine and seven, respectively—for two long years. Hugh was sent to boarding school, of course, and Mabel was shipped off to a small farm in Wales. No doubt the idea of the farm came from her father, a sensitive and understanding man, who had been troubled by his little girl's constant painful war with society as represented by a nanny, by any rule or regulation, by any "planned activity." Perhaps wild Wales may have seemed to this imaginative creature an entirely suitable landscape for his wild little daughter to roam in, happily set free from all that had bruised and harassed her in the genteel atmosphere of home. She was to be given the gift of solitude at this very early age, and though it would seem to us now a rather daring gift, how right he was! I know what a radiance of remembered happiness crossed my mother's face when she spoke of Wales, as of some lost Paradise, and what this long period of solitary communion with nature did for one who was always a discerning and passionate observer of flowers, trees and animals—one who would later have to remake her home many times among strangers, and twice even change her nationality. But the English woman in her accompanied every change, translating itself into gardens wherever she went, into the creation of beautiful surroundings, and, too, into a kind of impassioned solitariness. So what happened to her at seven in Wales was a preparation for much that was to happen later on.

Gervase Elwes and his wife were not wholly aware

of the particular environment into which they put their daughter so casually when they went off to Canada. What happened was that at the last minute the family with whom all arrangements had been made for Mabel, was unable to take the child; the Elweses, on the brink of departure, had to accept the word of these comparative strangers that they had found ideal substitutes. But the original family, as it turned out, was simply doing some poor relatives a good turn by providing them with a little extra income. Mabel's foster parents turned out to be two women—"Grannie" of the kind wrinkled face and kind hands, and "Aunt Mollie," her daughter, a tall, high-strung woman with eyes as blue as a jay's feathers, who, it appears, took an instant dislike to "the rich little girl." Even Grannie, of whom Mabel grew so fond, showed her no real affection until later. They were hard, primitive people, who perhaps regarded the child as primitive peoples regard "the foreigner" (she was English, they were Welsh)—as someone primarily to be exploited. Even so, it is hard to comprehend why one of the first things the two women did was to take away all Mabel's best clothes and give them to a nearby relative. There is, curiously enough, no reference to this astonishingly cruel behavior in my mother's written document. But though my mother did not choose to remember it when she came to write the story, it made an indelible impression on me as a child—so much so that I feel forced to place it in the record here. I remember very well my impotent rage at not being able to go back in time and tell those two women what I thought of them. I remember begging my mother to assure me that when her parents finally came back and rescued her, they did something violent and drastic, but she could not recollect that they did. Perhaps Eleanor and Gervase Elwes ended by feeling pity rather than anger, though my grandmother's irascibility was well known, and my memories of her include her shaking a fierce umbrella at a carter whose horse looked underfed, and threatening him in no uncertain terms with the law. At any rate, the whole story left in my mind a sense of incompleteness, of justice not done, until I read my mother's mature judgment of it and began to understand that, in comparison with all that followed of so much deeper human significance, this initial harshness may have seemed irrelevant.

Besides, memory distills the essence, and the essence of this whole experience for my mother was being alone in the country and all that that meant to the person she was.

Photographs of Mabel Elwes at this time show a pretty child with large wide-apart gray eyes, at the same time mischievous and dreamy, and light-chestnut curls piled up on her head. There is plenty of stubborn will in the mouth and chin. For her, Wales meant first and always escape—escape into lush meadows and an orchard in deep grass, and, above all, escape to the lovely shallow river, which ran bronzing over flat stones. At one place, she found a grassy bank quite close to the water, where she could lie for hours on her stomach and let the current flow through her hands like a constantly renewed spell; it was a forbidden game, and all the more delightful for that reason. In the orchard, a step up the hillside from the vegetable garden just back of the farm, lived Daisy, a greige-colored Jersey cow. Daisy allowed the little girl certain privileges; for instance, she could lie against the cow's warm flank when she rested in the shade at noon, chewing her cud, sometimes turning to gaze out of liquid brown eyes, without astonishment, at the small human being at her side. In return Mabel spent hours at a time whisking flies off the cow with a green branch. She spent hours, too—more arduous ones—pumping and carrying pails of water to fill Daisy's trough. It was quite a trick to make the water come—first by using short strokes in rapid succession, then by pulling the long pump handle slowly up and down. She could not carry a full pail, of course, and this meant that she had to make many trips before the trough was full. It was sad that after this effort Daisy always refused to come and drink right away, and would only do it in her own good time. But she had her moments of affection, when she followed Mabel wherever she went, even to the point of getting stuck between two hedges on a narrow path and standing there for ages, placidly chewing her cud, refusing to back up. They were both contrary characters, the little girl and the cow, but they respected each other.

In my mind's eye I see my mother running through those two years (how fleet her step even when she was in her seventies!) —across dappled light and shadow, always green leaves over her head and sunlight splashing down, alone with the cries of birds and the swift, shallow river. She wrote, "It was as if my mind and heart had been tied up with hundreds of careful strings and these were suddenly loosened and fell away. O marvel, O inexhaustible dream, O happiness!"

But solitude is one thing and loneliness is another. She was at times cruelly lonely. The two women used, for instance, to go out at night to play cards with the neighbors some distance away, leaving the little girl to suffer such agonies of fear as only those who have experienced them can imagine, while she sat shivering in the dark at the top of the stairs, quaking at the hoot of an owl or the creak of a branch, until at last—sometimes as late as midnight—the footsteps on the path meant that she was saved. Grannie, it is true, "grew fond" of her "in the end" and could be "trusted." How fearful to remember that Aunt Mollie could not—this presence fearsome in its reserve and strangeness, like some goddess who could not be placated. It was Aunt Mollie who looked coldly at the child one day and said, "You have a mean little mouth," inflicting one of those wounds that rise up to haunt a lifetime; my mother winced visibly each time she remembered it, as if she really wondered to the end if it were true, as if she had been marked by it, and some childlike sense of herself as the beautiful being she was had been poisoned there and then, forever. Aunt Mollie was the creature of moods, sometimes humming and singing all day, then suddenly sullen, with a sullenness that might break out any moment into violence when she moved about the house exactly like a thunderstorm, banging the doors, and filling every corner with her darkness. At such times, sensible people kept out of her way. As a matter of fact, those angry fits interested Mabel very much, for she had had tantrums herself, and knew how difficult it was to control them. She remembered how her father had taken her on his knees during her outbursts and tried to help her. He had taught her to go off by herself at such times and hammer out her rage against a piece of wood with a hammer, or break sticks, letting the seizure play itself out against inanimate objects. So now on the dangerous days at the farm Mabel watched warily, and kept silent, or conferred with Daisy, or took long aerial rides in the orchard, where a swing had been set up for her and she could imagine she was flying.

No doubt Gervase Elwes's vision of the farm in Wales had included good country meals, fresh eggs and milk. The reality was rather different. Eggs were a rarity —most of them went to market—and those custards dear to English hearts were fabricated with something called Canary custard powder. On Sunday evenings, the three at the farm had a small glass of fresh milk each, as a special treat, for the milk, too, had to be sold for cash. But there were compensations. My mother always remembered and spoke of the breakfast bacon, which was broiled in long strips that hung from a tin contraption set upon the live coals of the grate. It tasted delicious. Sometimes there were also mushrooms, collected before breakfast in the dewy grass. The child's great unsatisfied craving was for sweet things. Sugar was kept locked up in a glass-doored cupboard, so she got into the habit of sneaking into the kitchen, getting up on a chair, and dipping a finger into a can of sweet condensed milk that was kept on the top of the stove, then greedily sucking off the sweetness.

One day, Aunt Mollie came in as she was at this stolen pleasure. Aunt Mollie was in one of her fits. She yanked the child down by the hair and shook her violently. Then, as the paroxysm rose to its climax, she banged the can down on the table and forced the child's face on it, again and again, till her mouth and cheeks

[ *31* ]

were badly cut and scratched by the sharp tin edges. "I'll teach you, you thieving little brat!" It took Grannie's sharp command—the one word "Moll!"—to break the terrifying atmosphere of uncontrolled rage. The possessed woman pushed the child away, laid her head on the table, and gave way to long, retching sobs. Mabel, too frightened to cry yet, just stood there, licking the scratches around her mouth, while the old woman went over to her daughter, laid a hand on her shoulder, and said, "Moll, my poor Moll, what have you done now?"

Mabel had been too shocked to feel pain, but then the scratches began to hurt rather badly and she cried out in her distress. At last, Grannie led her away, washed her face gently in warm water, and then sat for a long time in the parlor with the little girl in her lap, rocking the grief away and leaning her head now and then on the curly one, as if to rest a burden there. At this point, Mabel began to enjoy the drama of the situation and to long to talk about it. She felt that she had some experience of such matters, and wanted to explain about the hammer and sticks. The old woman smiled down into the earnest face rather sadly but said nothing, and just rolled the child up in a blanket and left her on the sofa to have a nap—left her feeling a little jealous, for it was clear that Grannie's thoughts were elsewhere.

Somehow or other, this scene cleared away some of the resentment that had no doubt been building up in Aunt Mollie since the intruder arrived. For quite some time afterward, she was gentle, once even touching Mabel's face with a tentative finger, as if to ask whether the scratches still hurt. There was a change in Grannie, too. She found little ways of showing the child affection

—a piece of sugar hidden in Mabel's apron pocket, or a glass of real milk by her bed at night. It seemed almost as if all would be well.

At this time, Mabel was entirely absorbed in a new companion, a bedraggled, starving kitten that she had found one day on her rambles and brought home to care for and feed. It was a miserable sight at first, so dirty that one could not tell what color it might be, but it soon licked itself clean and emerged a tiny tabby with every stripe in place. Aunt Mollie disapproved strongly of the whole affair. But Grannie said the child could keep the cat, provided she trained it herself and cleaned up after it meanwhile. At last, the little girl had something on which to lavish affection, something that responded, something her own.

Then, one unlucky day when they were all away for some time and the kitten was left locked up alone too long in the house, it chose Aunt Mollie's room to be dirty in. When they came back, Mabel's first thought was for her kitten, but while she was still looking around for it downstairs, she heard a scream from upstairs, a sound of running feet, and then a high, mounting cry of distress from the kitten as it flew through the air and fell at the bottom of the stairs with a soft thud. Aunt Mollie got there before the child could, caught the kitten up as it tried to crawl away, and, holding it by the nape of the neck, made as if to beat it against the wall. Mabel, suddenly beside herself with rage, flung herself at Aunt Mollie like a wild animal, biting and kicking and screaming, "I'll kill you!"

They did not see Grannie, but, clasped together in fury as they were, they felt her there, standing silent at

[ 33 ]

the door, as the kitten crawled off and hid under the cupboard. Locked in that strange embrace, they turned, frozen by the presence of the quiet old woman. She still said nothing, only leaned her head against one hand on the frame of the door. Then she gave each of them in turn a long, piercing look that, my mother wrote, "made me feel older and Aunt Mollie seem childish." There was no scolding. Mabel was sent upstairs to clean up in Aunt Mollie's room. The old woman turned to her daughter gravely: "Moll, I have to talk to you . . ."

How dreadfully quiet a house in which violence has taken place seems when it is over. Upstairs in her attic room, the child waited. Finally, Grannie came, bearing a glass of milk and a piece of cake on a tray; there was another glass on the tray, for by this time Aunt Mollie had also been sent to bed. "The kitten is all right. One leg bruised, that's all. No bones broken."

Hours later, Mabel woke, feeling certain that she had heard a door open and the stairs creak. She sat bolt upright, listening, then crept out to discover that in fact Aunt Mollie's door was open. Panic seized her. Had Aunt Mollie gone after the kitten again? The child stole down the stairs on bare feet, guided by a faint light from the kitchen. There was no sound. She crept along the hall until she could see through the crack of the half-open door. What she saw was the woman kneeling beside the kitten's basket, holding a small saucepan of milk to warm over a candle on the floor beside her, her empty glass nearby. Her face was blotched from crying and looked inexpressibly forlorn and wretched. After a very long time of this tense silence, the milk seemed warm enough to be poured out into a saucer. The kitten meanwhile was

[ 34 ]

sitting up in the basket, watching all this as intently as Mabel did. But it did not move when Aunt Mollie held the saucer out, whispering, "Come, kitten, come." The kitten was sleepy, and Aunt Mollie was not good at cajoling. (Would she get impatient? Mabel wondered with terror.) At last, it made up its mind, stretched stiffly as it came out of the basket, shaking the bruised leg as if to unkink it, and settled down peacefully to lap the warm milk. Aunt Mollie reached out one finger to stroke its back, very gently. At this point, it was all Mabel could do not to cry out, "They don't like to be touched while they are eating!" Indeed, the kitten stopped lapping, withdrew a little, twitched its fur where the finger had touched it, and then—Oh, relief!—went back to the saucer again. Mabel crept back to bed full of bewilderment and a painful wonder.

A few days later, Grannie told the child that a doctor was coming to see Aunt Mollie, and that Mabel was to play out of doors and keep out of the way while he was there. The little girl went down to the swing in the orchard, and swayed slowly back and forth, chanting songs she had made up. She was called out of this dreamy state of contentment by Grannie's voice, shrill and anxious, asking her to come right away; the doctor wished to talk to her. "What does he want?" Mabel asked fearfully, as she walked toward the house at Grannie's side. "I'm not ill."

"Tell the truth, child," the old woman said sternly. "That's what he wants."

It was all rather solemn, taking place in the parlor, a room always dim because the geraniums in the window shut out most of the light. The doctor was sitting there, a large, fat man dressed in black, his knees spread wide and, between them, a small table with papers laid out upon it. He looked out at the three with a hard suspicious look, and Mabel took an instant dislike to him, comparing him in her written account to a piece of cold fat on the edge of her plate, which it made her quite sick just to imagine. "Stand here," he commanded, pointing to a place just in front of him, as if she were a criminal. He asked her name and age, and wrote them down. He asked her how long she had lived there—but how could she answer this? There had been no time in Wales; it was forever and a day. Grannie, after some calculating, answered for her, "Seven months." This voice from the other side of the room caught the child's attention, and she turned to look at the two women, sitting there, at either end of the black horsehair sofa. Aunt Mollie was gazing steadily over the man's bald head at the geraniums in the window. She was behaving as if he did not exist.

In the story as my mother wrote it, it is not clear whether this doctor was an official personage, sent for, perhaps, at the request of a neighbor, or whether the old woman herself had sent for him, torn between responsibility for her small charge and for her troubling, troubled daughter, and hoping to have a terrible decision taken out of her hands. Whatever Grannie had had in mind, it is clear that by the time the doctor arrived, he was not welcome. That grave command: "Tell the truth," laid a heavy burden on a seven-year-old; in fact, Grannie was putting the decision up to the child.

The doctor rapped out the next question with a knock of his glasses on the table: "Are you happy here?"

"Of course I am," Mabel answered crossly. She felt a very contrary mood coming on.

"And are you never afraid of your Aunt Mollie?"

"No, never," Mabel said, without a second's hesitation. She did more; she went over to the sofa, sat down beside Aunt Mollie, and slipped a hand under the woman's arm and down into her hands, folded in her lap—a gesture so extraordinary that it could only have been called out by extraordinary circumstances. But the child sensed that he was trying to get her to take sides against Grannie and Aunt Mollie, and, whatever happened, she was on their side. So there they sat, the three of them lined up on the sofa, and he, the enemy, watching them. Deprived of whatever dreadful secret he had come to ferret out, the doctor snapped his spectacles into their hard, shiny case and got up to go. Grannie escorted him stiffly and politely to the door, and in the second when their backs were turned, Aunt Mollie glanced at Mabel, and the child saw something like a twinkle come and go in those blue eyes, in an instant's humorous exchange of triumph. Was it a recognition of loyalty, perhaps? Or perhaps, at long last, love? Never again did the woman hurt the child, although she still had stormy door-banging days.

How often we talked, my mother and I, of going back to Wales someday and finding the little valley, the lonely farm, the orchard, the swift, shallow river—even, perhaps, the hazel hedge where Mabel and her brother, when he was there for the holidays, had once cut out a secret hiding place. We never did. But perhaps such vivid memories need no renewal in time. They are there, curled up like Japanese flowers; one has only to dip them into the waters of consciousness for them to open and fill the heart. So it was for me when the story of what really happened in Wales was superimposed upon the glimpses I had had of that time as a child. Some of the sheen went, as I read through those pages in my mother's hand, which tell in detail all that I have written here, and something harder and deeper took its place. Now, thinking of my mother as she was when I knew her—of her compassion and of the fire that blazed up in her whenever injustice was done, of the startling and wholly unsentimental truth of her perceptions—I think of the little girl in Wales who learned so much through such unconventional means. It was not dreadful or wrong at all, what happened to her there, but a time full of secret riches, which she understood because she was already the person she was to become, able to face reality, and to face it with complete courage, on her own terms.

*Raymond Limbosch*
*"...that world of their youth in Ghent..."*

*Mabel Elwes and*
*George Sarton*

## The Fervent Years

When they spoke of that world of their youth in
Ghent, my parents always had the same look, tender,
amused, and somewhat astonished as if it seemed even
to them not quite believable, a little miraculous perhaps,
and also a little absurd. The fervor, the innocence came
back in a phrase, an anecdote, told always with merri-
ment, but elusive—it was apt to be followed by a sigh,
for the world of their youth was the pre-1914 world,
and it vanished forever with the First World War.
Through their laughter or that shy look of complicity
they exchanged, I could recapture a gleam, an atmosphere only, but now, since their deaths, it has become
extraordinarily haunting and clear to me as I wander
—as tender, amused, and astonished as they—through
the letters and journals where it remains a living legend.
I hear my father cry out, at nineteen, "*Oh, n'avoir qu'un
coeur!*"—Only *one* heart with which to feel, think and live
all he imagined! When my generation looks back on
their generation, we feel old; they seem forever young.

How to evoke it? The point in time, the point in
space? There is one episode in the early 1900's before

my mother appeared on the scene, that brings it back for me in all its charm. On this occasion young George Sarton closed the door of his father's house behind him and set out to walk along the canals and through the narrow streets toward the Minard Theatre where he was going to hear a lecture by Anseele, the socialist leader. The stiff high collar, black boots and formal black suit concealed a shy, eccentric, passionate young man. His eyes were mischievous, quickly filled with tears, always bright behind thick glasses. Every now and then he stopped to jot down an idea or a phrase in one of the notebooks he carried for the purpose. He had recently published, in a privately printed edition of one hundred copies, his *Songerie No. VII Notammant sur le Bonheur et la Gloire;* the reader was not informed that "Songeries" one through six did not exist. And George Sarton had very little idea of either glory or happiness as yet, for he was in a perpetual fever of ideas and feelings that had no outlet. "Friday," he noted in his journal, "was a bad day: a gay sun in the morning and the sight of several young girls whom I thought pretty completely upset me." The books by his bedside were Pascal, *The Imitation of Christ,* Hello, Maeterlinck, and Fromentin's novel, *Dominique.* He spent his days writing and reading, yet he reminded himself in his journal that next year (he would be twenty-one) he would undertake some scientific studies at the university, "in order to get into closer touch with life." There was no sign of the dedicated scientist and historian, except that cryptic comment in his journal, a journal that bore the title *The Non-Conformist:* "I believe one can divide men into two principal categories: those who suffer the tormenting

[ 40 ]

desire for unity and those who do not. Between these two kinds an abyss—the 'unitary' is the troubled; the other is the peaceful." He still thought of himself as a novelist and poet, but the longing for a unifying philosophy was already there in seed.

Naturally, all these things considered, the Non-Conformist was not in the least surprised to find himself making the acquaintance of a delicate-looking young man of his own age, in the seat next to his; a young man dressed in corduroys and whose hands, though sensitive, were obviously those of a workingman, a workingman who spoke French, unusual in this part of the country where Flemish was the common speech. But this vagary was soon explained by the fact that Raymond Limbosch, who had by now introduced himself, had studied at the *Ecole d'Agriculture* at Montargis in France; he was presently working as *"ouvrier horticole"* for the well-known firm of de Smet. George Sarton, hungry for friendship, and especially for friendship outside his own milieu, warmed to the occasion, and invited Limbosch to dinner the following night. No doubt George described this chance encounter enthusiastically to his father on the latter's return that evening from the usual coffee and liqueur at his club. And no doubt Alfred Sarton smiled a little skeptically but assured his son that this new friend would be welcomed and put at ease.

The two young men saw each other frequently after that. Limbosch was an anarchist, Sarton a socialist; the socialist-anarchist dialogue took them through endless walks about the city they hardly noticed in the heat of the discussion. They soon found that they shared an interest in poetry. Sarton recited verses by Francis

Jammes and Verhaeren (just then coming into his fame) and Limbosch answered with the whole of de Musset's *Nuit de mai*. They ended up in a café, to smoke and drink coffee. It was only natural that Limbosch invite this new friend to come and spend a weekend with his own family in Brussels. He had spoken of his mother as "involved in lingerie," and Sarton imagined some small local shop in the village of Rhôdes-St. Genèse; it would be an adventure to experience the life of these simple people.

The firm of Limbosch was actually very grand, a *"maison de haute couture,"* designer of trousseaux for the nobility; the peasant interior George Sarton had imagined turned out to be a large country house, in a fashionable suburb—though at that time there were still rolling wheat fields all around it, and, nearby, the magnificent Forêt de Soignes, miles and miles of soaring beeches pruned and cherished ever since it had been set aside as a hunting forest for the Dukes of Burgundy. Sarton walked from the trolley stop and was hot and dusty when he finally discovered the Avenue Lequime, but he still suspected nothing, and decided that possibly Raymond's mother worked in the house as a maid. He thought of going to the back door and wished that he had done so when the front door was opened by a butler. I can see him, his mouth slightly open, his look of innocent astonishment, when the truth finally dawned.

There is something about this story that recreates for me the perfume of that moment in time, its unrealistic idealism, its liveliness, and its gentle irony, for although each of these young bourgeois was sincere, each was playing a part to the hilt—the anarchist-gardener for whom a butler opened the door when he set out each morning with his dinner pail, and the ardent young socialist who imagined that all workingmen were "pure" and noble.

It was not only youth that made it possible for George Sarton to note in his journal in capital letters "THE IMMEDIATE BEAUTY OF LIVING!" For he had come to the point where for a brief period his powers reached out in multiple directions, where he could live all the sides of himself in a way that would not be possible once he knew what his life work would be. Now he was a poet, a novelist; he was also an active socialist; in January of 1905 he confided to his journal: "After two years of anxiety and uneasiness I have returned to socialism. I shall do all I can for the socialist cause, because I believe that opinions that do not translate themselves into action are dead, useless opinions. I do not believe that the socialist state is the ideal; it appears to me as simply a step towards anarchism, for which men are far from ready today. Socialism will lead them there, by making men good, generous, and just." And by the next year he had embarked on mathematical studies at the University. Above all, he had found at last a few real friends, not only Raymond Limbosch but the effervescent medical student Irénée Van der Ghinst, a real *copain* at last, an enthusiastic non-conformist, and a young man so "pure" that he dazzled George Sarton and filled his friend with naïve admiration. No longer would desolate cries appear periodically in the journal: "Always alone, wholly dependent on myself, desire, the thoughts that devour me. O my God, give me a friend to be near me. I no longer have the strength to be always alone; there

[ 43 ]

are moments, sinister hours when books and engravings are no longer enough companionship. . . ." Confession of an ardent young man of twenty that one cannot read without smiling, but whether God heard this desperate plea or not, at any rate Irènée and his enthusiasms must have seemed a good deal more real than any book. Together they founded a student organization called *Reiner Leven* (Purer Living), the purpose of which was to lift the brutalizing level of student life and provide a center for those who did not look to prostitution and liquor as major outlets for their energies. The group arranged lectures on history, politics, art, vegetarianism, went on excursions and picnics in the surrounding countryside, or carried on discussions in their "local" which was, significantly enough, The Temperance Café.

At the same time the same ferment was alive in a group of working girls from a more modest social background, girls who did not attend the university, but instead the *Ecole Professionnelle* of the city of Ghent, a business school that trained them to be secretaries and clerks. They, too, had formed a club, and called themselves the *Flinken*, an untranslatable Flemish word meaning "merry" or in French, "*gaillard*." Their language was primarily Flemish; their parents were small tradesmen, butchers, grocers; but just like the university students, the children of the "*petite bourgeoisie*" were in revolt against their background, were fervently committed to plain living and high thinking, though their seriousness was tempered by a good deal of laughter and self-mockery. They were ardent feminists of course, called each other by surname, and believed that wives should support themselves. One of them, Marthe Patyn, already had a job as secretary to the firm of Dangotte, interior decorators, and so was responsible for bringing into the *Flinken* two young women of the bourgeoisie, Céline Dangotte, just entering the family business, and Mabel Elwes, a young English artist who was living with the Dangottes as a daughter of the house.

The *Reiner Leven* young men were unaware of the existence of a sister organization until they put an ad in the paper, for the purpose of recruiting new members at the university. The *Flinken* saw the ad, signed Irènée Van der Ghinst, and supposed that Irènée (spelled rather eccentrically with two final "e"s,) must be a woman. The *Flinken* despatched a pretty young woman called Mélanie Lorein to go and have a talk with Van der Ghinst She was delighted, of course to find that "the young woman" was actually a charming, fanciful young man. Van der Ghinst reported the affair to Sarton and they agreed that nothing could be more appropriate than to include a group of working girls in *Reiner Leven*. It was a fairly daring departure from the social mores of the period and no doubt this fact added a certain pleasure to the whole affair. They went on regular Sunday expeditions together, walking through the country with knapsacks on their shoulders, singing the *Internationale*. Each member in turn was assigned a subject upon which to talk to the assembled company once a week at the Temperance Café, and sometimes professional lecturers offered their services; for years these meetings were held with great regularity. In 1906 and 1907, for instance, I find noted a lecture by Professor Hoffman on vegetarianism, a lecture by Dr. Pelseneer on the exploration of the floor of the ocean, by Professor Bruyon on the plants of the region (this was in Flemish); by Dr. Willems on ants; by Céline Dangotte on Fitzgerald's translation of Omar Khayyam; by George Sarton on workingmen's universities in France and England; by Mabel Elwes on the pre-Raphaelites. On other occasions there were discussions on such questions as collectivism, the sense of duty, fraternity between the sexes, the eight-hour day. When it came to lectures by their own members, George Sarton was prodigal of advice and encouragement. Thus when Mélanie had to prepare a lecture on Breughel, she received a postcard, courteously written in Flemish, saying simply, "Lorein will speak very well because she wills it," signed Sarton.

George Sarton, who had for so long looked longingly at pretty girls on the street, was now surrounded by a whole bevy of them, who teased him unmercifully, laughed at his clumsiness, and were a little afraid of this eager mentor who wrote them long letters suggesting that they embark on all sorts of studies. He invited Mélanie Lorein to work with him on mathematics so that she could get her high-school degree at night school. After an hour or so of study, Mel would find herself sitting opposite George in the formal dark dining room of his father's house eating yoghurt, raw carrots and nuts and trying not to smile at the incongruity of this ostentatiously frugal meal, and the bourgeois surroundings—trying, too, not to smile, at the solitary child he was, for the old servant would have placed a *tartine*—a bread and butter sandwich—at his place, as she had done every evening since his babyhood.

Again I find the essence of an atmosphere, a moment

in time, in a letter George wrote to Marthe Patyn in 1907.

"My dear Patyn,

"If it were really impossible for you to study a subject seriously, it would be absurd for me to ask you to do so. But I am convinced that you have the ability to make a fruitful study of a social question: it is simply a matter of perseverance and of good will. Only thus will you acquire a *method* of thought. And if one cannot reproach anyone for being ignorant of this or that—for ignorance is not a sin—it is legitimate to reproach someone with poor reasoning. This rigor, this scientific sincerity is only achieved by the attentive study of a specific subject. If I suggest a social subject, it is precisely because these are the only subjects that can be approached without a foundation of knowledge. . . . And besides, haven't we all the fervent desire to help in however small a way, in the progress and freeing of humanity? And to act efficaciously, one must *know,* and in order to know, one must *study.* So if you truly love mankind, if you really long to hasten the reign of justice and love, you will arm yourself for the good fight, by *studying.* Besides, sociology remained for a long time outside scientific investigation, which means that there are a great many social questions that have not yet been *completely* explored; and that is another encouragement. . . . I am ready to consecrate to this a large part of my time. Don't be afraid to ask my help; I shall be *inexhaustible.*

"You know that I have resolved to study the relations between 'Masters and Servants and the condition of domestic servants.' I have already assembled some notes for this work, and read some articles.

"If this subject pleases you (it is easy to study), let me know when we can have a talk about it; for it is too long to explain by letter. I'll give you all the indications possible. And by working two hours a week, in five or six months, you will understand this matter better than anyone in the world.

Fraternally<br>
Sarton."

It was then and later one of George Sarton's charms that he projected his own wide interests onto friends and companions, and naïvely imagined that what delighted him must delight them. When Laurette Willem, the daughter of a professor at the University, was eight and George in his twenties, he gave her a copy of Fromentin's novel, *Dominique*, and when someone protested that the book could hardly interest a small child, he answered "but *I* love it." So it was that a series of magnificent dictionaries was presented to me at Christmas and on my birthdays (notably the Harrap French-English tomes) but found their way into George Sarton's library. It is probable that Marthe Patyn never did make a study of the relationship between masters and servants, but then, neither did George Sarton. She was feeling her way towards her true vocation, that of becoming a nurse; and he was beginning to narrow down the range of his studies to mathematics and chemistry, at least temporarily, for he still considered himself to be primarily a creative writer and in the next years published, privately, under the pseudonym of Dominique de Bray, two romantic novels that were rather more like moral treatises than anything else, *La Chaine d'Or* and *Vie d'un Poète*. Besides all this, he was not unexpectedly falling in love with Mélanie Lorein.

It is here that my mother enters the scene, although neither she nor George had the faintest idea what role she was finally to play. She entered it first as the confidante, for in this world of "comrades" where personal matters did not go unnoticed or undiscussed, there had been some alarm about George's growing interest in Mélanie. He was twenty-two, and ultra-romantic, from a totally different background than the much younger girl, and they all felt that it would be dangerous for him to declare himself before he was sure, and that he had perhaps been swept off his feet and risked sweeping Mélanie off hers before she was ready for marriage. Quite a crisis brewed up in July of 1906; letters were exchanged; George had a long talk about his problem with Céline Dangotte, and the results appear in his journal as follows: "I love Mélanie Lorein, but I have promised my friends Céline Dangotte and Mabel Elwes to say nothing to her before October, for fear of troubling her young soul. I have promised, and she shall know nothing. Is she the woman I shall love all my life, and who will share my existence? She draws me to her, and charms me by her mystery and the tranquility of her eyes.

Tomorrow I leave for Holland to see Rembrandt."

The solitude from which George Sarton had suffered from his babyhood on was at an end. For he was off to Holland with his intimate friend, Irènée Van der Ghinst, he had two charming young women with whom he could begin to feel at ease, whose advice he could ask, whose tender concern he needed desperately—and his romantic nature had found a focus in Mélanie.

What of Mabel Elwes? Strangely enough, she was going through a reverse of this experience of his. As his life began to come into focus, hers was to suffer every dislocation and tragedy, and the independence and courage she had learned as a little girl in Wales would come to the test again and again. Her relationship with her father had been an especially close one; Gervase Elwes was a Fabian, an agnostic, a highly intelligent but unworldly man, with a delightful sense of humor and adventurous courage. At twenty-four, before his marriage, he was building bridges for one of the first railroads in the Himalayas, and the same spirit of adventure led him later in his life to make risky investments in mines. By the time his daughter Mabel had been educated (she was sent to a finishing school in Ghent), his affairs were in a bad way. It was clear that Mabel would have to earn her own living as soon as possible, and to that end she was sent to the Black Heath Art School where she learned to do miniature portraits. By the year of 1906, when she first met George Sarton, she was a professional portrait painter, and was also doing some interior decorating for the firm of Dangotte. It was not easy to make ends meet, but she was just managing. In August of 1906 she had gone home for a holiday; in the middle of one morning her Uncle Ernest appeared, in a state of shock, and said, without preamble, "Your father's dead. Where are the keys?" And when she had managed to understand what had happened—Gervase Elwes died very suddenly of a heart attack, brought on by his financial worries—she had to go out into the garden where her mother was sitting, and break the terrible news to her. In a brief interval this girl in her twenties had to face the loss of her father and financial ruin, for Gervase Elwes had concealed from his adored wife and from his daughter and son, that he had lost his entire fortune in the Rhodesian mines. No doubt he had counted on being able to recoup in one way or another, but the fact was that his family found themselves destitute. All of this was made more painful by the fact that Mabel and her mother had never been intimate friends; Nellie Elwes was primarily a wife, not a mother, and though she gave her heart to her only son, she did not come to love her daughter until she, Nellie, was a very old woman.

But fortunately Mabel's heart had already been transplanted to Belgium. There Madame Dangotte and her daughter Céline offered her a home, the most tender, loving care and understanding, during the time, after this shock, when she was seriously ill. Most important of all, Madame Dangotte had faith in Mabel's talent, gave her work to do, and that supportive belief more precious than money.

I never knew Madame Dangotte, alas, but I have a strong sense of her personality, dogmatic, fiery, temperamental, and generous. She really ran the firm of Dangotte, for during these years her husband was withdrawing into a life apart from his family. Three small images of her float up into my mind: The first is very small and precise; whenever she noted that Mabel looked depressed or when things were not going well for one reason or another, she would lean over the table and say tenderly, "Mabel, *prenez une poire*" and this little phrase, "Mabel, do take a pear" became a family joke, used whenever any one of us needed cheering up. The second image is an example of her kind of generosity, spontaneous, utterly unlike the bourgeois world where pennies are counted and drawers are locked. I remember my mother once describing how much she longed for a new dress on the occasion of her first exhibition of miniatures in Ghent, and Madame Dangotte, with a wave of her hand, telling Céline and Mabel, "Go to the cash register, my darlings, and take whatever you need!" The third image evokes the atmosphere of the period, as well as Madame Dangotte herself. For tradesmen were still beyond the social pale, and when Madame Dangotte bought a carriage and pair and was seen in the streets driving around like a member of the aristocracy, she was stoned. However she was not deterred (she too was part of the ferment of the time). After the first few dangerous *sorties* her carriage and pair, and the indomitable courage that held the reins, were allowed to pass.

Let me for a moment evoke this young woman, Mabel Elwes, as George Sarton glimpsed her, when she began to emerge from the dark time after her father's death. He writes to her in October, 1906 (he was twenty-two and she was twenty-nine),

"My dear friend,

"While walking yesterday afternoon I suddenly caught a glimpse of you leaning on the arm of Céline Dangotte; I recognized you both from far away: you were passing the Place du Commerce at about 2:58. I was so greatly moved that I went home as fast as I could. Irènée Van der Ghinst has kept me in touch with the state of your health; but now that I have seen you in the street, that is to say more or less well again, the idea came to me that I might address myself directly to you without indiscretion. Give me some news of yourself, will you? That would make me very happy. I suppose that you can occupy your mind during the day—reading and looking at the reproductions of paintings that you love. You ought to read amusing, gay things: do you know the *Bruxellois* dialect? If you do, you must read *La Famille Kaekebroek* by Courouble: it is a book that amused me so much that I forgot to work for a whole day. But I'm afraid you would not be able to understand it. Just as English novels have always remained incomprehensible to me. A while ago I read one of Kipling's books, *The Light That Failed*. In the abstract, I admired the book very much, and I wanted to read it all, but *physically* speaking it was sometimes so repugnant to me that I had a wild impulse to throw it out of the window. I don't know if you can understand all this—at the moment I have begun to read Upton Sinclair's *The Jungle* but I don't know if I shall finish it, because, having received a dozen books from different people, I began them all at once, so as to be through with them more quickly! Am I not idiotic?—Good. Now you are laughing—and that consoles me a little for my foolishness.

"I thought you might occupy your leisure by perfecting your French. That is why I am sending you an excellent manual by Courouble, where you will easily learn the subtleties, and elegant phrases of our language." [This, of course, was a joke as Courouble was a humorist who wrote in dialect.]

"I hope with all my heart, that you will soon be altogether well.

Your devoted<br>Sarton"

It was the beginning of an ardent and argumentative correspondence, ardent in its longing to communicate with each other on a deep, but not at all amorous level, argumentative because Sarton and Elwes disagreed hotly about a great many things, and notably the pre-Raphaelites, whom Elwes admired a good deal more than he did. It is moving to me to learn that they began as friends, the kind of friends who demand a great deal of each other, who confide in each other, and who learn from each other because they are each passionate in conviction, and able to express themselves. It is time, perhaps, to allow Mabel Elwes to speak in her own voice, and this is simpler because by early 1907 her letters to George Sarton were in English and need not suffer translation. He was at this time still struggling with his feeling for Mélanie Lorein, and confiding in Mabel Elwes as a friend. I have chosen this particular letter out of a great many because it seems to me to give a portrait both of Mabel Elwes herself and of their relationship in its beginnings.

28, III, 1907

"Sarton, thank you for your letter, thank you for trusting me enough to choose me when you need to talk to someone at times. Please never hesitate to do so. I understand so well how you must feel sometimes—(at least I *imagine* that I understand!)

"My first letter to you about Mélanie Lorein? I remember so little just what I said? I remember I was

[ 54 ]

frightened of writing to you, quite dreadfully frightened, but something drove me to do it. I was frightened partly because I had so little *definite* to tell you, almost all I wanted to say was based on feeling and instinct and I was afraid I should do no good perhaps—just muddle you even if I succeeded in arresting your attention. At the same time I felt a danger approaching both Mélanie and you—for her I had real sympathy already though I really knew her very little, and for you real esteem, though I knew you 'secondhand' chiefly through Céline, and so I felt it was due to you *both* to say what I thought.

"*Oui* [Here the letter continues for a few sentences in French as inscribed here.] *je le sens que vous avez fait du progrés vers le beau, vers le bien—je pense à vous parfois avec une admiration qui vous étonnerait et vous amuserait même un peu peut-être*—but let me say so once, though I know that the opinion of your friends is not a factor in your *motives* of action, still, unless you are less human than I suppose, it must be a sort of comfort in difficult days, to feel that there are people who trust in you, who realize some little part of your struggle, who are happy when you succeed. Oh Sarton, Sarton, there is something in you that I like so much—I seem to be always arguing and disagreeing with you, but indeed, in spite of that, I feel that you are not such a horrible long way off from me as almost everyone is from everyone else. Now will you understand what I mean? I really can't explain, it would take so long.

"And I too think that Mélanie is *wonderfully* pretty —'wonderful' is just the word that expresses what I mean. Her eyes are full of 'wonder' and there is something indefinably *pure* in her face—I catch myself staring at her

[ 55 ]

sometimes till she must wonder what I am thinking of her, but she is very unconscious—something still of the real childish unconsciousness mixed with a certain womanly dignity. And she has such a beautiful forehead—I don't see the good of telling you all that—either you think the same, or else you think something different and will disagree!

"I do believe that you manage to think me even a little narrower in my interests and a little stupider than I really *am*. On the other hand, the question of the future of human society has interested—even fascinated me, even given me periods of morbid fears and nightmares! for years and years! Where you are perfectly right is when you think and say that I have never studied anything with sufficient system and perseverance. I *loved*, ever since I was about fourteen years old, to *talk* of these things—religion, sociology, and many other questions, with my father—and to please him, and to be able to understand what he said, and to be able to understand and express what I felt—which was by no means *always* what he felt!—I read a fair amount—but I was the most irresponsible 'insouciante' girl *on the whole*, that it is possible to imagine. I have always loved life, loved the sun, the earth, and everything on it and above it so intensely, that it took up most of my time. I had fits of melancholy when I used to make myself ill (oh feminine exaggeration and inconsequence!) by realizing all the suffering that existed in the world and then I got scolded for giving away all my dolls in a lump or doing various wild and foolish things (I am not penitent! I learnt something each time, and I should be sadder now if my thoughts of those days had never led to any *action*, however impulsive and unreasoned). I tell you that because it is a sort of indication of my present failings! but I too have struggled—I have really made an effort to 'sort up' my feelings in such a way that they may lead to good to myself and other people—which means that I have tried not to let them run away with me—(I have not always succeeded.)

"Yes, yes, I know what you mean by *"se transformer progressivement, harmonieusement"*—I like that expression, it is indeed a summing up of what to *really live* means.

"Good night, my friend, do you know you are one of the only men I know, with whom I have no trace of that feeling of 'distrust' any longer—not that I think you perfect—but—well, you understand I hope.

Yours sincerely

E. Mabel Elwes"

During these years, 1906–1909, George and Mabel corresponded with each other far more regularly than they actually saw each other—Mabel describing at length the family with whom she stayed in England to do a portrait in June of 1907, George answering with a report on his work for an examination in preparation for his thesis in chemistry. He tells her, "it seems to me that I would work with far greater ease if I had before me a reproduction of Donatello's St. George. I think about that St. George all the time." So it was quite natural that Mabel Elwes find one in London and send it to him. By such exchanges of imagination they were slowly and almost imperceptibly being joined by a hundred invisible threads.

Meanwhile it was spring for others in the group. The

horticultural workman, Raymond Limbosch, was turning into a poet, and was falling in love with Céline Dangotte. Again I find a letter written in fading ink on a disintegrating sheet of scrap paper that opens up and sets before me with perfect vividness, the atmosphere of one of the outings of the *Flinken,* to the Dangottes' country house, *Les Assels,* along the Lys near Ghent. It is a letter from Raymond to Mabel, Mabel the friend to whom he had written shortly before to ask, "Do you think I am really a poet? What do you think, you who are in the family the calm beam of light?" It is a letter full of the recognition of love and the peace of it, but also, it seems to me it comes down through the years as an image of the time and of the place and of this particular group of romantic idealists:

"Mabel! My dear Mabel, if only you had been there, at the *Assels* on Monday! The happiness I carried away with me from that day! I cannot tell it to you: there are words but they cannot say what the heart feels. My heart lives in joy as in a fresh blue morning. Céline and I have created such a beautiful light between us. Veneration and peaceful tenderness. You were with us, Mabel, in our thoughts, all those who have done us good were with us. If you had heard us you would no longer have felt the artificial, the fabricated, the too wilful, in us. Oh, no! And our clear and peaceful understanding was lifted like a lovely stalk of wheat, in the midst of the discussions and the most idiotic jokes. . . . Then towards evening, the Flinken . . . sat around the edge of the pond and Céline and I read poems of the Comtesse de Noailles. Then supper where we talked only of conduct between young men and women, with wit, good sense, revolt, smallness, and meanness, quite a jumble! All this about Alice who was seen with a young man . . . but Céline will tell you all about that in detail. Then, a divine walk—Henriette, Céline, Augusta, Margo and Mariette and I—along the borders of the Lys. Mabel, the landscape of Flanders in the evening! What emotion! Then such dear words from Madame Dangotte that I have to hug her—then, a walk around the garden with Céline. Then the night, gentle, gentle, with the sound of the pigeons, then dawn, the morning, the garden. What a magnificent collection of columbines, Mabel! . . . How pretty and varied they are, I enjoyed them tremendously. The sweet peas are doing well, though mine have only just germinated. The peonies are beautiful; the bouquet of rhododendrons is in full flower; the first poppies are opening, the big red ones. The garden is so lovely, a little wild and savage as I like it best."

Mabel Elwes must have been happy to hear about the garden as it was she who had planted the columbines, and even now fifty years later I sometimes hear from Céline, that she has just planted this or that flower "that your mother loved." But for the moment Mabel was racing against time to get a design for lace into a contest, and could not join her friends at the *Assels*. Some days later she is writing to George, "I worked all day Saturday except for a half hour at lunch-time, on the design for lace that I am sending to the *Concours de la Chambre Syndicale*. Yesterday was the deadline. Will I win a prize? I hope so because I am broke, dead broke, but even if I don't, I enjoyed making the design, and I learned a lot besides, about the technical problems to do with execution. I feel that there are such lovely things to be done with lace. Why do the women who make it have to go along like machines executing only one or two designs during their whole lives? They have no pleasure, it must be almost maddening, it seems to me. I would like to create a whole lot of new designs using plants that these peasant women know and try to make them understand and love what they are doing—"

During the following year, Mélanie Lorein fades from the scene, and it is clear to everyone that the friendship between George and Mabel is ripening into love. But it was not to be a gentle passage for either of them, and in the two years that followed there was much painful heart-searching on each side. Their intimate friends were incensed at the kind of pressure George brought to bear; they were anxious about Mabel's health. It was common to the general ethos of the group to believe that men and women are equal and must support each other, but nevertheless George's categorical statement in his journal when he was still magnetized by Mel had in it an element of exaggeration (as well as an apparent total disregard of the responsibility of a father toward any possible children) that explains the violence of Raymond and Céline's initial reaction to the turn things were taking, for George noted in his journal: "Lorein knows that my wife will have to be ready to be the wife of a pariah, a pariah herself; and that in no way will I undertake the support of my wife: at least she will have to be prepared if necessary to support herself." Mabel was valiantly trying to support herself by all sorts of designing and crafts that were not what she really wished most to do—to be a painter—but she was finding it hard going. During these years she had several opera-

tions and spent months at a time unable to work at all—
and she was also sending a regular sum toward the support of her mother. Her friends argued that marriage,
which would involve children, the running of her household, as well as her own work, was more than she had a
right to take on. Everything brewed up to crisis just as
George passed his oral examination toward the Doctorate
in Newtonian mathematics and went off to London for
a month to celebrate. He wrote in his journal: "I passed
my examination pitifully: the first ordeal toward the
doctorate in physical and mathematical sciences. It made
a very painful impression on my professors and will do
me a lot of harm at the final examination. I have learned
nothing this year that has moved me or influenced me
very much." But he had not been idle, exactly, since he
had not only prepared the examination in mathematics,
but finished his thesis in chemistry and written a novel!
At any rate, this first trip to London proved to be a
revelation—he was enthusiastic about the parks, the
museums; he discovered the Fabians and began to read
Wells and Shaw and to feel that Fabianism mitigated in
a constructive direction, "our doctrinaire Marxism," but
he was even more articulate on the subject of the English
woman: "What a marvelous race! I have rarely seen more
beautiful human beings than the slender distinguished
women I saw in Hyde Park or in Piccadilly. It has
changed my whole aesthetic of the human body. I love
also the energy and independence of these women, their
decided air; certainly I shall do all that's possible to
marry an English woman, and that, soon, because I want
very very much to marry: I am tired of being alone."

Although she is not mentioned by name, and perhaps the relevance of his description was unconscious, there is no doubt that the image of Mabel Elwes is there just behind these vivid impressions. However, this long passage, which celebrates George Sarton's twenty-fifth birthday on August 31, 1909, ends with the tragic paragraph: "I have said nothing in these pages of my friend Mabel Elwes. Our situation was hopeless. After having hoped and despaired three times, I have become convinced that she will never marry me: she is too jealous of her independence; she lacks the sublime fath of Jane Welsh. So I have broken off my relations with her, because they had become impossible. It is for me an immense pain, and I shall not be cured until I love another woman. Alas, I can neither foresee or even hope for such an eventuality. My heart is, as it were, broken. But my life is not."

In the autumn of that year Mabel Elwes fled to Zurich, ostensibly to study at the *Kunst Geverbe Schule*, but really no doubt because to be in Ghent and near George Sarton had become too painful. They did not communicate with each other, but for each it became in memory "that terrible year." And the photographs of Mabel Elwes at this time show a face locked inwards in grief, though she was, as always, absorbed in her work and could write to the *Flinken*, "I love my work. I am finishing my first piece of bookbinding and am sending it to you as proof of my affection."

Mabel came back from Zurich as from a long journey in the desert of the heart, and in that early spring of 1910 these two passionate, sensitive, opinionated, strong characters came to admit that they could not live without each other, and, forgetting entirely what he had said in a moment of disillusionment, George noted: "I might say of us what Carlyle said one day of Jane Welsh, 'Has not a kind of Providence created us for one another? Have we not found each other? And might not both of us go round the Planet seeking vainly for a heart we could love so well?'"

This chapter has been a celebration of a group of friends launching themselves into life, and so it is not surprising that even the Sarton-Elwes engagement was due to the intervention of a friend, Madeleine Van Thorenburg. She and Mabel Elwes had been the first two women to be allowed to draw from "life" at the School of Art in Ghent. No one could have been more gentle than the shy, discreet Madeleine, who took no part in the activities of the group, was not a member of the *Flinken,* and lived a cloistered life (because of ill health) among her family: her father was a distinguished wine merchant. But it was Madeleine who took Mabel by the hand, and said, "Go to George, he will never come to you, but he loves you." And on the first day of spring, the day Mabel appeared in the little studio of the old Dominican convent taken over by artists and scholars where George had a study, they became fiancés and celebrated the event by hiring a boat, rowing down the Lys, and eating an engagement luncheon of asparagus and hard-boiled eggs, in true Flemish style. The long rich wanderings and digressions of youth were over. In this same month George Sarton speaks for the first time in his journal of what was to become his life work. "As soon as I have my doctorate, I shall try to get a post at the university, and meanwhile I shall finish my studies abroad. I shall probably become the pupil, if I prove worthy, of Henri Poincaré: the most intelligent man of our time.

"I hope thus to become more than a writer of fine phrases, and bring my effective aid to the progress of the sciences. It is almost certain that I shall devote a great part of my life to the study of 'natural philosophy' (*philosophie naturelle*). There is great work to be accomplished in that direction. And—from that point of view—*living* history, the passionate history of the physical and mathematical sciences is still to be written. Isn't that really what history is, the evolution of the human intelligence; the development of human *greatness*, as well as its weakness?"

And some weeks later, on the thirtieth of May, 1910, shortly before his marriage, he had come to a firm decision, even at the risk of having no permanent job, and no visible means of support: "I have decided now, as soon as I have the doctorate, to devote myself to my own work without further preoccupations about getting a stable position. That exclusive need for security did in fact seem to me suddenly a cowardice:—to work, let the chips fall where they may! Mabel thinks as I do about this; and it's not she, God knows! who would turn me from my ideal."

*"'Wondelgem,' the name itself sounded like magic to me as a child."*
*May, two years old, is at the left.*

# Wondelgem: The House in the Country

Two houses stand behind me—one, my grandfather's somber house in the city of Ghent, where my father grew up; the other, all light and sunshine, the country house three miles outside, in Wondelgem, where I was born. "Wondelgem," the name itself sounded like magic to me as a child. It was part of that faraway paradise "before The War." It was quite literally in another world, since I did not remember it myself (I was two and a half when we left Belgium), a little girl who, in Cambridge, Massachusetts, heard the peculiar tenderness the word evoked in my mother's voice, as if the walls of the tiny apartment where we lived opened out at its sound into a secret garden, into a still airy house with roses climbing all over it, and inside, the walls covered with books.

It had been bought by the sale of my grandfather's wine cellar after his death; connoisseurs, many of whom had sat at his table, were at the same time scandalized that such a sale should take place at all, and delighted to be "in" on it: they paid high prices, and the result was a small fortune. Instead of water being turned into wine, in this instance wine had been turned into strawberry beds, into a small orchard, into great oaks at the bottom of a long green lawn, into the dear house itself, and its gradual furnishing with cupboards, tables, beds designed by my mother and made under her supervision. Never mind if she and her young husband slept on mattresses on the floor for three months while cabinetmakers lovingly polished the bird's-eye maple and walnut, fitting together the patterns in the wood so each piece seemed in the end to show the opened heart of the tree. It was all alive, this house and garden in the process of creation. Belgian workmen thought my mother crazy when she insisted that the cold frames be dug to a depth of four or five feet, but the English green thumb was a determined thumb and she had her way. While she saw to the planting of gooseberry bushes and red currants, and mixed borders of flowers with the vegetables in the *potager*, my father unpacked boxes of books and measured out the shelves in his study where the *History of Science* ("my own invention" he might have said like the White Knight) was being born.

They must have each of them stopped sometimes in the middle of a morning to lift their heads and smile, and find it still unbelievable that this dreamed-of house and life was theirs, together, the penniless English artist and the young Belgian scientist, who had taken so long to make up his mind about what he wanted to do that, at one point, one of the formidable uncles said, "You have put yourself beyond the pale, and you will never get a job." Only four years before, Mabel Elwes had written in one of those long exploratory letters they exchanged: "We passed by your house yesterday afternoon, and I looked at it. It had a sad look to me, the look houses have where there have never been any children. I have a very clear and painful image of you as a child, then as a young man, struggling, alone, in that somber house, where I felt nothing of the light and radiating atmosphere that certain houses have, an atmosphere that enters into hearts and minds and helps them in their lives—an atmosphere illuminated by the presence of affection, of a happiness quiet but penetrating, a reassuring atmosphere." And when, a few years later, their engagement was announced, it was not only Mabel's friends who had their doubts—George's Oncle Arthur could say to him, "I do not need to tell you, I am sure, that the announcement of May 23rd startled me.

> 'Must one weep or must one laugh
> At such a solemn moment?'

That is the beginning of a piece of verse that my father and your grandfather sang at the wedding of Uncle Joseph of Douai.

"Indeed, your fiancée is in poor health and probably without fortune, while you, without much of a fortune, are going to face great difficulties in attaining any position because you are a free-thinker, a Mason and President of the Socialist Students in a Catholic country, where the Catholics will be in power for a long time to come.

"You know this as well as I do and that is why you are converting into pennies, one after another, all the material assets of your father.

"You are making your opening move, on the gambling table of life, without the two great trump cards which are conditions of happiness: health and money."

But these were not the questions that Mabel and George fought their battles over during those years when they argued so fervently and at such length over the pre-Raphaelites, for instance, or the sexual mores of Belgian youth at the time, over woman's independence, and once a battle royal over the conditions of divorce in case they did marry, and decided to separate! True, she was never very well, and had had a serious operation and a disturbingly slow convalescence shortly before they were engaged. But what she knew already, even if he did not, was that the nervous tension that brought on migraine headaches and made her heart beat too fast, was also the strength on which she could depend in any crisis, a strength that would help carry her and her husband through whatever lay ahead, a fierce and joyful will so that—to name a single instance—she could lie down in the garden path for a few seconds during labor pains, and then get up and finish putting in the strawberry plants, until it was a race between her first baby's arrival and the job that she did just finish in time.

There in Wondelgem at last, full of their own dreams, the young married couple paid no attention to Oncle Jules Sarton, the retired army captain, who was writing articles to the papers to point out that it seemed rather strange that the Germans were building huge railway stations and junctions so near the Belgian border. For what are these designed, he asked pointedly? But no one bothered to answer, except to tease him about his King Charles head. In those days, only a little over forty years ago, war could be still considered an anachronism, medieval madness which nineteenth-century Progress had made impossible. People planned their lives for peace. Deep in the country, under the shade of the oaks, my tall slim mother was sewing at the printed linen curtains, so strong and delicate they would last a lifetime. The blue flax from which they had been made waved in the fields along the Lys. And my father wrote letters to scholars all over the world announcing that he was founding a review to be devoted to the history of science and civilization. *Isis*, as it was named, was born in the spring of 1912, and Eléanore Marie, as I was named, shortly after. My father always referred to us together and dedicated one of his books to "Eleanor Mabel, mother of those strange twins, May and Isis." By now my name had shortened itself. The "comical" baby as my mother called me, or "Extra-sec" as my father somewhat ironically called me, lay in a basket flounced in pink and white dimity on the floor where the fifty-page pamphlet formally introducing *Isis* to the world, lay ready to be folded and mailed.

It was to be, as its editor hopefully defined it, "at once the philosophical journal of the scientists and the scientific journal of the philosophers, the historical journal of the scientists and the scientific journal of the historians, the sociological journal of the scientists and the scientific journal of the sociologists." It was such a huge idea that it never occurred to young George Sarton that the response might not be commensurate with the dream, or that, far from helping to solve the financial problem, *Isis* turned out to be a good deal more expensive a venture than its twin. "We were innocents," my father used to say. But perhaps he did realize even then that innocence and fervor such as this are in themselves "trump cards."

As I grew up from a basket to an outdoor crib, my father's notes for the *History of Science* grew in their boxes, and the garden was growing all the time. There were expeditions to the antique shops of Ghent to look for old pieces of Flemish furniture, beautiful in their heaviness, in the lustre of the dark wood, in the twisted columns which supported a table or adorned a cupboard —a "bahut" as it was called. Friends came out "to spend a day in the country"; I was carried from flower to flower in my mother's arms, reaching out (so it seems) even as quite a small baby to the color and scent with ravished eagerness. The dramas were small dramas—my first independent adventure, escape from the crib and a crawl to the strawberry beds where I was found red with juice, delighted with what the world outside had to offer; or, the trickle of answers and subscriptions to *Isis* which grew to a hundred, but that small company was already a sign of the journal's international appeal, and even included one Indian Rajah!

My English grandmother came over for a visit and inadvertently became the first occasion of what turned into a family joke, our fatal ineptitude about meeting each other at a train or boat. Grannie was not timid, but she spoke no French, and it was quite an adventure to cross the Channel alone. George was to meet her at the station in Ghent, but somehow they missed each other, and he apparently panicked, and simply disappeared into the city for several hours, while Mabel in Wondelgem waited anxiously, and Grannie sat in the station in a state of alarm that gradually changed to fury, for she had a very hot temper. I'm afraid she must have thought it typical of "a foreigner" but it was actually only typical of George Sarton's incapacity to deal with mundane affairs, or perhaps simply another form of "innocence." For if material matters became too disturbing, his invariable technique was to pay no attention. If the cellar flooded, for instance, he would say with a philosophical smile, "Let nature take its course." But I still sometimes wonder what he did during those hours and hours between his abandoning his mother-in-law, and his sheepish return home, to find she had finally taken a cab and was already there.

It must have been shortly after her visit, that the young couple decided to invite all my father's uncles and his Tante Hélène to come out for the day and see for themselves how their eccentric nephew had installed himself and his family. It turned out to be one of the hottest July days on record. The Sarton family were lovers of good food and wine, and at this time my father and mother were vegetarians and teetotalers. The family, as we know, had their doubts about George's English bride; their ideas of interior decoration were Victorian. The whole thing must have been something of an ordeal for all concerned, so what was my delight to discover the other day, an enchanting letter from the bachelor Oncle Arthur, who seems to have been completely won over, not only to *Isis* and Marie (my name had not yet reduced itself by one syllable) but to the whole ambiance of the young Sartons' lives! He writes in a delicate spidery hand on expensive paper, and the whole letter looks like a "composition," no doubt copied off from a rough draft. It reads:

[ 71 ]

"Your debuts, my dear George and my dear Mabel, that have just made their appearance, are dramatic coups and master strokes.

"Vegetarians by principle and by training, you met head on the cortege of carnivores that we are, all of us together brandishing the flag of fish, winged creatures, and ruminants.

"True, you softened the brutality of the gesture by providing us with delicious delicacies and the most refreshing fruits.

"May I be permitted, while on the subject, to apologize for the insatiable thirst (satisfied at once, I must say, and in the most charming atmosphere) I exhibited from the beginning to the end of my visit; but it was so hot, and I suffer then from inundations of sweat and an inextinguishable thirst! If hell exists and I am destined to go there—as seems probable—I shall certainly not enjoy myself.

"But you at least will have passed your noviciate in hell—you and Marie, of the thick hair, laughing with her brilliant eyes—in the enchantment of your honeymoon and of your pa and maternity, in an earthly paradise far from troublesome people, and those formalities and social obligations that imprison.

"What pleased me very much was to find that your dwelling, far from appearing to be a bric-a-brac shop, has become a 'cottage' [Oncle Arthur uses the English word], though I might have preferred a verandah with frosted panes instead of the open trellis, throwing light on the whites and pale colors of the paintings and hangings, on the furniture (perhaps slightly rectilinear but original), made of strange woods, beautifully worked, and decorated with medallions painted by the mistress of the house—the comfort of hot and cold water in abundance, lighting, bells and ventilation, all instantaneous.

"We are certainly in England and not at all in the stuffy antiquarian atmosphere of Ghent.

"I find your garden unique, relative to its small extent. It is wooded like a park, better than the forest where the trees, once full-grown, retain only the bole and the crown. I still see in my mind's eye a purple beech, large and leafy as a larch. Great and beautiful trees are the masterpieces of nature; they people the landscape with moving shadows; they are the ancestors and inheritors, binding together the generations. To them we owe the song of the finch, the lark, and the blackbird, warblers and nightingales in the leafage; it is the great trees that shelter your lawns and flowers from the incendiary fire of the sun; they are also, by the trembling of their leaves, precursors of the storm, of which they are, alas, sometimes the victims. Great trees should be regarded as sacred objects.

"In a vegetable garden I have myself never seen any flowers except tomatoes, broad beans (that scent the air), peas, many peas bearing through at least three seasons, beans ('princesse de Sabse'), many beans and strawberries, white and red, Vilmorins and ever-bearing. I have always excluded potatoes; they take up a lot of room and always give an inferior product in volume and quality compared to those grown in the great airy spaces of the country. I planted pear trees and apples pyramided along the sides, gooseberries, black and red currants. I also had beds of asparagus and hot-beds, first for chervil, radishes and early lettuce, later for melons.

"But I am chattering on, and I forget, my dear George and my dear Mabel, that all this, cottage and garden, where I have been losing myself, the reunion of old and excellent relatives, of which I have said nothing —and that is a mistake—was steeped all the time in the charm of your affection, always alert, always smiling, affection that will remain engraved on my heart."

This letter must have meant a great deal, for it was kept through all the upheavals, one of the few family letters that survived. Perhaps, later, in the dreary board-inghouse in New York where we lived as refugees for a time, it came back to my mother as it did, the other day, to me with a whole past in its old-fashioned scent.

Meanwhile in Wondelgem in the spring and summer of 1914, we were beautifully happy and independent, all three. My mother was busy designing the furnishings of a room for the firm in Brussels for whom she worked, a room to be shown at the international exhibition of Arts and Crafts due to open in August. She had made a trip to Austria to work with the craftsman responsible for the inlay of wreaths of flowers in brilliant colors, for this was not done in Belgium. Belgian craftsmen, on the other hand, were polishing the bird's-eye maple a smoky blue, and bringing the insides of drawers to a satin finish. She had designed the rugs, the curtains, the pillows, as well as the furniture, which was amazingly modern for the period, and would seem modern now but for its rich decoration.

I had my fierce ambitions and desires, too. Once it came upon me with violent certainty that I must have a bowl of goldfish exhibited in the window of a little shop in the village. I was dressed in a white coat and hat, in white shoes and socks, and when this wholehearted need was denied me, I flung myself into a mud puddle in revenge. I had tantrums, but the doctor's remedy for them—to plunge me into a tub of water fully dressed—I treated as a delightful game; I loved flowers and my mother passionately. I was a little frightened of my father who used to throw me high in the air and cry, "Wa wa! Wa wa!"

In late June my mother was absorbed in the final stages of her creation, the embroidery on the emerald green curtains, and the making of the rugs. On June twenty-eighth, the Archduke Ferdinand was assassinated. All through July, as my father worked quietly in his study, and my mother wondered why the plum tree again this year looked as if it would not bear, diplomats hurried back and forth across Europe. War, which no one would look in the face, which was called "a scare," lurked around the corner. The papers were filled with rumors, and my Oncle Jules grew apoplectic with rage, as he tried to warn his cronies in the cafés of Antwerp.

Preparations of a sort were made, but halfheartedly still. The Civil Guard, to which my father at one time belonged, drilled now and then on the village green, and took uniforms out of mothballs. Sometime in July they were issued ancient muskets. But no one really believed in that impossible war as a reality. In any case, they reminded each other, Belgium itself was neutral. Nothing could happen here.

On August second, the Germans demanded free passage, were refused, and on August third the Wehrmacht marched in in their spiked helmets. In the little village of Wondelgem church bells rang the tocsin; the postman delivered mobilization orders. My father, though no longer an official member of the Civil Guard got out his heavy Civil Guard coat, took down the old musket, and reported for patrol duty. He was set to guard the railway intersection. There, alone, a lantern in one hand, his gun in the other, he paced up and down all night hoping that the German army would not come hurtling down the track. Fortunately, they did not.

What followed is confused in my mind. Bits and pieces of the tales so often told float up. The Belgian armies resisted valiantly, but it was an improvised war and no one knew just what was happening. In the retreat from Antwerp an officer friend—it was Irénée Van der Ghinst—turned up exhausted, filthy, hardly able to speak, had a bath, and then went on to try to find the remains of his regiment. One night my mother started up in terror as a series of explosions rocked the house, but my father said, "It's just the Germans blowing up the bridges," turned over and went back to sleep. The next morning he decided on the spur of the moment that he must go to Brussels and offer his services to the Red Cross as a stretcher-bearer, was turned away after standing in line with hundreds of other volunteers, and then went over to the Institut de Physiologie with the same purpose. One gets an idea of the confusion from a penciled note he wrote my mother, and it is interesting to realize that apparently the mails were being delivered in the middle of this chaos! "I have been on duty here at the Physiological Institute for the last two hours but this duty consists essentially in doing nothing; everywhere there are more people than are needed. We are expecting wounded. Seventeen have already arrived (there is room for eighty), but I have so far seen the arrival of only two. Most of the men brought to Brussels are not really wounded—but rather footsore or exhausted.

"I have had no reply from Headquarters and don't expect I shall now. So I intend to come back on Monday. I haven't come back sooner because journeys are difficult and painful at the moment. I have several times already been suspected of spying!

"So, unless something happens before then, I shall be back in Wondelgem on Monday. And probably I shall take up my work again. For I fear that it will be the same story in Ghent, *i.e.*, that there are ten times too many people for each job, and thus overcrowding. For instance Raymond stayed at the station yesterday from five P.M. to two A.M. to pick up in all two wounded. Again because there were ten times more cars than needed.

"In these conditions, I think it is more courageous to direct my energies into another channel, with the idea of volunteering again if there is real necessity.

"Everything is very depressing here——"

My father's abrupt departure, leaving his wife and child alone in Wondelgem (the maids were no use at all; they put their aprons over their heads and wept without ceasing), and his decision to come back again after three days are as good an image as any of the general panic and dislocation. Meanwhile the gray flood of the victorious Wehrmacht was sweeping through, many of the soldiers as bewildered as the populace. The fruit was ripe on the trees at Wondelgem (all except the plum which for some reason, remained infertile) and at a five-minute break a group of soldiers started climbing over our wall to steal. This was too much for my English mother's sense of decency. She ran out, her eyes blazing, and berated the invaders in no uncertain terms. I was often told as a child how sheepishly they scrambled down, like children crumbling before the unmistakable signs of authority, and went on their way. Twenty-six officers and men were billeted on the place a few days later. One officer, looking over the quarters, walked through while my mother's heart nearly stopped beating as she suddenly remembered the Civil Guard coat hanging on the back of a door. At this time members of the Civil Guard were treated as spies and shot. But she was able to push the door back and stand against it, and that night the coat was buried in the garden. One of the officers was rather human, and admitted that he had no use for this war; another knocked over the pan of milk warming for my supper on the stove with a brutal gesture; one of the soldiers went all through his pack to unearth a square of chocolate and take it upstairs when he heard me crying. The whole situation was chaotic. For on the one hand, unexpected kindness might be shown, but on the other my father was held responsible for the nineteen men and if one of them had not shown up at curfew time, he would have been taken out into the garden and shot—and there was one traumatic night when this appeared to be about to happen.

Little by little my mother and father came to the decision that they would have to leave the country. My father became convinced that he would be more useful doing his own work, and this seemed clearly impossible in Belgium. But money was frozen in the banks. Passports to Holland, which had remained neutral, and from where the Sartons hoped to reach England, were extremely hard to obtain. Even when all the interminable waiting in offices in Ghent had been accomplished and we had the necessary papers, how to get there? We had to be prepared to walk with only what could be stuffed into my baby carriage. But in the end we did manage to get a horse. What to take? "Just this book," George would plead, and a pair of shoes was dumped out to make room. The boxes of notes could not go; they filled a small metal trunk which my English grandfather had used in India, and this was buried, late one night, in the garden. At last the few suitcases and a trunk were strapped onto the carriage; and we set out for the border, passing through the advancing army. There had hardly been time to take a last look at the garden, at the beloved house, lying there so airy and sunny and quiet in its orchard green. Did my mother look back one last time at the long protecting wall that had sheltered all she loved for such a very brief time? At the great beech, standing inviolate, its leaves shining in the sun?

I remember none of this. It still sounds like a fairy tale, a fairy tale which, after all, after many tribulations, ended well, since no one died, and it came full circle at last in another deep green garden in Cambridge many many years later, a garden which had no great beech in it but instead a little wood full of wild flowers in the spring.

My memories of the house begin and end on one day in 1919. This day stays with me like some marvelous strange dream when you are allowed to go back in time, but everything is curiously distorted. I was seven. Until then Belgium had meant to me the postman hurrying up the path a year before saying, "Mrs. Sarton! Mrs. Sarton!" and handing her those first letters with Belgian stamps after the four years of silence, and my mother sitting down, tears streaming down her cheeks, unable even to open the letters, only knowing, "they have survived," the friends who had been imprisoned behind the wall of suffering while we, the earliest and most cherished of refugees, slowly found ourselves and our new life in a tiny apartment on Avon Street in Cambridge.

Now we were on our way back to Wondelgem. How did we get there? By trolley from Ghent? By carriage? Like a dream this journey has no beginning. We are there at the gate. The first thing we see, even before we go in, is the barren plum tree, laden with huge blue plums. I can feel all through me my mother's beating heart. We push open the gate, and are in Sleeping Beauty's garden. It is all so still, so lush, so overgrown that we have to cut a path through tall yellow flowers to reach the house, but the house stands. It is there, waiting somehow proudly in spite of two bomb-holes in the roof, and the wild jungle of green thick growth all around. Everything feels ripe and breathless. It is very hot. Fruit everywhere—cherries, peaches, plums (have I invented this?)—looks like fruit in a dream. One hardly dares to touch it, for it may not be real. And I am nothing, an observer, nothing but eyes. It is my father's and mother's moment, the long poignant look back into the lost past.

Inside we are met by chaos and filth, chairs broken up for firewood, rubbish knee-deep in the corners, desecration. Through these patient walls armies had flowed back and forth, making do with what they found, and if it happened to be a fifteenth-century chair, well, someone else would break it up if they refrained. At first, my mother and father must have felt only their life together violated, trampled down, made ugly and filthy in every possible way. The dream, so beautiful and mysterious while we stood outside, had turned into a nightmare. I opened a cupboard and saw on the floor what looked like a heap of symmetrical cannon balls, but made of mud. What were they? Some madman's game? I have never forgotten them.

But just then my mother cried out, "Look, George!" She had lifted out of a pile of rubbish a single Venetian glass on a long delicate stem, so dirty it had become opaque, but miraculously intact. How had this single fragile object survived to give us courage? It went back with us to Cambridge and it was always there, wherever we lived. And now it is here, in my own house, a visible proof that it is sometimes the most fragile things that have the power to endure, and become sources of strength, like my mother.

The dream fades out into a story, perhaps a legend. It seems that two German officers lived in the house during the first two years of the war, and stole a girl from the village to work for them. She was never seen again, except once, glimpsed through the curtains of a closed carriage. That is all that is known. But it soon became clear that the officers had other amusements. All the German books on the history of mathematics and physics had disappeared. My father took down moldy dusty books one after another, opening them at random, to discover that they too had been violated. The officers amused themselves by tearing out an end paper here, an illustration there, until they had gutted the library, a methodical, not very amusing game, one would think. But no doubt they were bored.

I was beginning to feel frightened, as if we were ghosts, entirely unreal, and only the rubbish and desolation was real, when we heard someone tearing through the flowers. One of our peasant neighbors stood shyly at the door. She held out to my mother a pile of beautiful old plates.

"But where? But how?"

All these years she had stored them up, one by one, as the officers paid for eggs and butter with some object from the house. Never knowing whether we would come back, she had saved them; she had hoped; she had foreseen the possible happiness she might one day have in her hands to give back. Only then, with the dear old plates in her own hands, so clean, so brilliant, so untouched, so wrapped in human kindness, did my mother weep.

Later I must have been told about the precious notes, for it does not seem to be a part of that day. A distant cousin of ours succeeded in digging them up, safe in the metal trunk, and kept them toward my father's return. Like the Venetian glass, they survived, as fragile, more precious, since without them George Sarton could not have written the first great volume of his *Introduction to the History of Science*.

That is what I remember of Wondelgem, except the very end, and that I had almost forgotten. It came back with a rush the first time I heard the axes chopping down the cherry trees at the end of Tchekov's *Cherry Orchard*. I remembered. We went back to the house once after it had been sold like The Cherry Orchard to break up into small lots for villas. There was a strange noise like tearing silk and we saw that workmen were wrenching the climbing roses from the walls (they reached the roof of the house and were all in flower) and I heard my mother's desperate cry, "Couldn't they wait till we've gone?"

But that was not all. That day the new owners chopped down the great trees, those celebrated by "Oncle Arthur" as "the ancestors and inheritors, binding together the generations," oaks three hundred years old, "to get a view," the new owners said.

So the heart of the house was torn up by the roots and carried across the sea where little bits and pieces of Wondelgem gave a flavor to the house in Cambridge, an atmosphere that held balm in it, the balm that comes from continuity, from dear old things much lived with, like the old "bahut" with its beautiful twisted pillars, and the table with legs to match these, sturdy, dark, glowing. There was even—memory of that glory which never quite came to pass—one piece of the inlaid furniture my mother designed for the great exhibition that never opened. After the war, when the pieces were taken out of the cellar where they had been stored, and sold off, my father was able to purchase this one desk. We were hard up, and surely no jewel could have been more beautifully a sign of love than this fabulous object, too rich for our surroundings. It glowed softly in the dining room, and on great occasions it was opened to show inside the brilliant green leaves laid in the satin smoothness of the white wood, the mother-of-pearl butterfly, and the little secret drawers, so smooth inside they looked and felt like satin. It had not been designed for Wondelgem, but it has always seemed to me to carry with it the atmosphere of that house, so gay, so full of life, precious as a jewel that will never lose its radiance, so intense, perhaps, because the life there, rich in hopes and dreams, was so very brief.

## O My America!

The ship that left Liverpool at the same time as ours was sunk, and we turned back to pick up survivors. It was September, 1915. My mother and I were on our way at last to join my father in America; there, after a long year of refugeehood in England we hoped to be able to make roots. It had been a year of separations and heart-searching for my parents, for my father had first tried to get a commission in the English army, then considered volunteering as a private, and finally got a job as a censor in the War Office. But it was a time of hysteria, the war hysteria, and in this neither of my parents could share. It is moving to me to witness now that under the strain of the moment, they stood by their convictions. At the time when my father still hoped to get into the army, he wrote Mother, in December, 1914, "You will understand all my anguish of this week, if I simply tell you the conclusion at which I have arrived. It is this: what is worst about the catastrophes brought about by men themselves is that it is impossible to act wholly for the good (outside of the Red Cross) for violence calls out violence, and evil calls out evil. The act itself

*"In America, after a long year of refugeehood in England, we hoped to be able to make roots."*

of fighting is a monstrous thing; but what surpasses everything in horror and monstrousness is when the act of fighting becomes a moral duty, and the collective crime becomes for the moment the highest duty of the citizens." While he was trying to find his own way to what the right thing to do might be, Mother and I stayed with relatives and friends, as part of the flood of refugees from Belgium, welcomed so generously by the English. We were dependents, for the censorship job did not provide enough for us to live on, all three, and at last the decision, the immense decision was made that my father go to the United States alone and see if he could not find support there for his dream of writing a *History of Science,* and then send for us when he could. He left us in June, with a hundred dollars and a few letters of introduction in his pocket, and a still imperfect knowledge of English. Later he loved to tell the story of his student days, when he had (without any idea that this effort would become one day a necessity) decided to learn English, and bought twenty tickets at a Berlitz school, or its equivalent at the time. At the end of the first twenty lessons, he asked for another twenty tickets, but the professor took him aside and told him that he felt it would be dishonest to take his money as it was quite clear that he would never be able to learn and he had better stop trying! Here my mother was, of course, of the greatest help; we always spoke English at home, and for years she went over everything he wrote, until in the end he fashioned for himself a personal style that kept something always of French clarity with a dash of Flemish humor and an occasional foray into American slang, but which had a distinction that would have astonished his first teacher.

Now in September all that lay between us was the hazardous passage in the blacked-out ship. I was three and only dimly remember the Irish passengers singing hymns all night, the terrifying darkness where we lay in our bunks, in life preservers, waiting for morning. But at last we woke to the strong American sunlight, and a garden in Yonkers falling steeply down to the immense quiet river and its Palisades, on the opposite bank.

My America was, first, Teddy, a golden Saint Bernard who licked my face with a warm, happy tongue. The top of his head, rich and soft, lay under my hand, and because I was about his height, I could look straight into his eyes. He had a companion, a red setter named Buster, all angles and leaps, but Buster was too sudden to be a friend. Teddy and I went exploring down the steep lawn, arbored at the sides in grapes, to a vegetable garden interrupted by rows of sweet peas, and their intoxicating scent mixed with that of the ripe tomatoes, warm from the sun, that I stole and shared with him. Beyond the garden was a dangerous country full of poison ivy—an impassable barrier between us and another drop down to the river. I was severely warned about the poison ivy and its shining bright green leaves, tropical and sinister. America was not all safe and warm; the poison ivy suggested wilderness and danger. But there were chipmunks, and large gray squirrels with immense, full tails; there were huge robins, three times the size of our European ones.

How imaginative it was of the Baekelands—for the Belgian inventor and his wife were our hosts—to insist that Mother and I come to them first, and be cherished and spoiled a little before the serious business of our new life was attempted. Their house, rustic stone and brown shingles, with its turrets and verandas, its stained-glass windows, its large porte-cochere in front, and all surrounded by expanses of clipped lawn, seemed to me very grand. It had, for instance, a polar-bear rug in the drawing room. What luxury to compare with that of sitting on a polar bear's head? It also had a square glass aquarium, in which lived a small, wicked alligator who devoured raw meat and looked at me with indifferent, beady eyes. The real glory was the master bathroom with its huge bathtub. A bathtub? Rather, a tiled swimming pool, six feet square and sunk two feet into the floor. Around it lay huge sponges from Florida, and shells with rosy mouths that sang of a faraway ocean. In this bathtub, one could be a seal or a mermaid with no trouble. But that was not all. The dining room had a huge plate-glass window looking out across the Hudson and reflecting the dinner table at night, and near the ceiling there hung a little balcony. Long after I was supposed to be asleep, I could creep out there from the second-floor landing and lie on my stomach and peer down over the edge, through the balusters, to watch the grownups at dinner—my mother in some soft blue and green Liberty silk dress, which surrounded her English beauty like a cloud. My heart thumped so loudly on the floor I was sure it would be heard. Sometimes Annie, the waitress, caught my eye and winked, but the people at the table were looking down, not up, and I was safe. How beautiful grown-up people become at night!

My first human friends were Annie and the cook;

the kitchen, its windows at the level of the lawn, was my favorite place. Here I spent hours playing (was it then or a year or so later that we played "Hearts" by the hour?) and digging small, thin slices out of a round red Dutch cheese. There was also Dick, the chauffeur, who resembled Teddy in character but had the advantage of speech. Soon I was running up the gravel drive and turning off on the steep, hidden path to his white frame house to tell him about anything important, such as an invasion of huge, fat green caterpillars on a maple, or the discovery of a robin's nest—a fatal robin's nest, as it turned out. It was in the fork of a low branch of a small, thin tree, perhaps a birch, for it swayed when I climbed it. It was my first glimpse of a nest with eggs in it; there they lay, four bright, blue-green, perfect eggs. The mother was nowhere in sight, and I thought I would just borrow one for a little while to show Dick. But for once he was not pleased at all. He explained that now the eggs had been touched, the mother bird might never come back. His gentleness was worse than a scolding. For the first time in my life, I knew what it was to do something irrevocably bad. For the rest of the day, there was no joy in anything—not in sitting on a polar bear's head, not even in Teddy's company, because his innocence assailed me like a rebuke, and I really could not look into his eyes. I was fit company only for the wicked alligator, who ate raw meat and would probably have loved a robin's egg for breakfast.

Except for the maids and Dick—my true friends— only two other people seemed real besides my mother. I never did feel Dr. Baekeland as a person I knew; rather he seemed to be some frightening masculine force

—a god who must be placated, a piece of weather. I realize now that, with his fierce, shy eyes and black mustache, he looked something like Rudyard Kipling; and I realize now, too late, that, though I was frightened of him, he took me into his heart and really loved me in the admiring way of a grandfather with a first grandchild, for he used to come in after I was asleep and look down at me tenderly, and he was amazed that I could play so happily alone. But then, I fear, all I wanted was to run off and be free to go to Dick's house where I felt more at home. On my way there I passed the garage, and above it, I had been told, was the laboratory, a very secret and important place where Dr. Baekeland retired to work like a sorcerer, and no one was ever allowed to go. There he was busy concocting queer things in trays, rather like today's ice-cube trays, but the cubes were of a hard yellow translucent material, no good as toys, though he gave me some one day—no good for anything as far as I could see. The name of this invention was Bakelite, still in an experimental stage, and not yet the fabulous djinni it would become as one of the first plastics.

Bakelite did not interest me, but George Baekeland, our host's son, dazzling in his Air Service uniform, melted my heart. He tickled me and reduced me to agonized helpless tears of laughter. I followed him around as Teddy followed me, and his smile taught me all I knew then of passionate love. But his charms came and went, while those of his mother remained steadfast. She was known to everyone as Bonbon, a name so appropriate that it must have been used by St. Peter at the gate of Heaven, for kindness flowed from her in every sort and size of package, tangible and intangible. Her presence was a present. A small, round woman with bright, dark eyes under a mass of fuzzy gray hair, she wore for as long as I can remember the same round beaver hat and long beaver scarf over a suit she had recopied exactly each year. She could not have worn the beaver hat in summer, yet I see her so clearly in this hat and no other that she must be painted in it here. She came from an intellectual bourgeois family in Ghent, very much like my father's, but now she had moved into a different world, she had not changed. It was only that riches became her so well, as if she had always been intended to be a fairy godmother; she had the rare gift of transforming money into joy, her own joy and everyone else's, so there was no bitterness in it. Some of this I came to know later, but from the beginning she had my unwavering devotion because I sensed in her a dimension like saintliness, like poetry, which set her apart. Concrete evidence of this was the fact that because of her feeling for animals she would eat no meat. I loved animals, too, and even made resolves to follow her example, but then when everyone else at table except Bonbon accepted the breast of chicken or young lamb, apparently without a qualm, I forgot my resolve. (At this time my parents, who had been vegetarians in their youth, did eat meat. I have never known what changed their decision about this; perhaps it had happened in England where we would have only added to the burden of our hosts by requiring special food). Bonbon did not blame us cruder beings, nor make us feel guilty; that was her triumph. When she and I sat shelling new peas from the garden on the back veranda, Teddy at our feet, and Buster's red plume of a tail waving in and out of the grape arbor after a squirrel, I felt a wonderful sense of security and something like being at home, at least for a little while. I could talk to her, I found, even better than I could talk to Dick. I loved her Belgian accent, the way she said "Meerses" instead of "Mrs.," an accent that gave character to everything she said. She was very American in her lavishness, but she was also still so Belgian and so unsophisticated that she was, as I see it now, the perfect bridge from my Belgium to my America.

New York with Bonbon was Fifth Avenue, the Flat-iron Building, Woolworth's (at that time still *the* sky-scraper), and she had the newcomer's pride and delight in the city, as if, almost, it had been her own creation. New York was Best's where I suffered a mixture of shame and pride in being shown off as a "refugee," though pride triumphed when I was given a dark blue sailor coat with a red lining and brass buttons with anchors on them, as well as my first American shoes (which I fear I instantly hated), black patent leather with gray suede tops which had to be buttoned with a buttonhook. New York was sumptuous lavender boxes of chocolates from Sherry's with a scattering of candied violets on the top layer— those violets my father's extravagant mother had loved. And New York was the Plaza Hotel where we had tea among the palms, and ate little many-colored iced cakes, while, at Bonbon's request, the orchestra played a soulful rendition of the "Song of the Volga Boatman," and were rewarded with a crisp ten-dollar bill taken over to them on a silver plate. Perhaps I loved her so much because her taste remained the taste of a child, and her love of life, her excitement (as years later when she waved her hand at all of Yonkers glittering with electric lights and said proudly, "every one of those light bulbs has Bakelite in it") was as innocent as a child's.

The idyll in Yonkers could not last and soon we were facing "reality" in a dreary boardinghouse near Morningside Park. I remember nothing of that winter except my terror of the Murphy beds, for fear mine would shut up during the night, and my first experience of ingratitude when a squirrel to whom I had offered a peanut, bit my outstretched hand right through a white woolen glove. What I do remember is the atmosphere of anxiety as intangible as a cloud, but always there among us. My father was still searching for a permanent job; my mother was longing to find some way to help out. How moving it was, with this atmosphere in my consciousness, to find the other day this note in my father's journal: "It is extremely regrettable that the Europeans are so badly informed about conditions in America and about the ideal of this great people. I have conceived the idea of a big American institute in Brussels after the war (if Belgium is free again and independent!). This institute would have as aim to bring together all the documents concerning the United States and to distribute this information liberally. I am convinced that nothing can be more useful towards the peace of the world than the creation of institutes of this kind.

"The realization of this project would cost about $2,000,000. I'll do everything in my power to help to realize it."

Not only Bonbon was innocent! For here was my father, jobless, with a wife and child to support, launching vast projects—perhaps to keep up his courage. He never gave up his own dream, meanwhile, and turned down a good job as librarian at the Rice Institute because they would not meet his one condition which had nothing to do with possible salary, but was adamant: that they take over the publication and support of my twin, his review, *Isis*. He had a summer school job at New York University, I believe, and later on, he decided to accept a post at George Washington University in Washington, D.C. These were pieces of luck, as temporary measures. Even in those days when refugees were still (at least in the United States) single dramatic instances and not anonymous floods, it was not an easy thing for a young man, keen on going ahead with a task which could not possibly bear fruit for ten years, to find a way to support a family, especially when the young man had, in the process, to learn to use a new language. Nevertheless George Sarton held unwaveringly to the big dream, the writing of a *History of Science:* "We have been in exile now for almost a year. It seems to me I have accomplished very little during this year, but I have certainly learned a lot, my horizon has grown wider. I could do such good work, now!"

But he would not be able to begin, quite yet. Not for another hard anxious year. Washington never did feel like home. At night we could hear the wolves howling in the zoo nearby and somehow this sound haunts my memories, like the sound of loneliness itself, though people showed us much kindness. I was given a scholarship to a kindergarten nearby, called "The Little Potomac School," and there on the first day made a friend, Willem Van Loon, Hendrik Van Loon's son, to whom in the rapture of discovery I proposed marriage when we were sitting hand in hand on a washbasket—and for many years after we considered ourselves to be "engaged," till we were at least ten or twelve. At Christmastime a wonderful thing happened when Admiral Stockton left a large Teddy bear at our door, a Teddy bear to be embraced with almost the same passion I felt for Willem, and to whom I told long stories in bed.

Meanwhile my mother was trying to find a way to use her talents and help make ends meet. She had been a designer of furniture in Belgium, of course, and soon unearthed a carpenter in Washington who could execute simple designs, a cupboard for my toys first, and then a charming black cabinet, reminiscent of Japanese furniture with doors that opened onto shelves painted orange inside by my mother, and with a stylized design of birds and flowers on each door. I speak of it because it was for some time the only beautiful piece of furniture we had, and because it stands in my study now, a sort of household god that has meant "home" to me for all these years. Perhaps it was through the carpenter, I do not know, but in time Mother met a charming light brown lady, who was about to go into business, interior decorating, and wanted Mother to come in with her as designer. My mother learned something new about America when she had to recognize that, at least in Washington at that time, such an association was absolutely taboo.

The Washington year was not altogether happy, but it brought us our first American friends, and two rich and unexpected gifts. For my mother never found a way to go on designing furniture professionally, but she did form a business association which was to last for many years and to bear fruit in the firm of Belgart. My mother was the designer and her friend, Margaret Gillespie, the businesswoman of this firm, which created embroidered dresses and coats, using designs based on peasant embroideries, executed in bright wools and silks. Mother had always made my clothes, simple in cut, always with bloomers to match, in lovely colors and decorated with birds and flowers at the neck. Already in our brief stay in Yonkers and New York she had taken orders and made dresses for friends who saw and admired these. Dr. Baekeland himself had been much impressed and told my father, "These little dresses are so simple, sensible and beautiful. . . . That is the kind of art that I understand. When she created them, Mrs. Sarton did a greater thing than if she had produced the most beautiful painting—it is really a *great* invention. If now Mrs. Sarton did not leave anything else behind her in this country, than this idea, that would already be enough." My mother would certainly not have agreed with the remark about a painting, but she did greatly enjoy making these designs. She trained a group of women to do the embroidery, and Margaret Gillespie ran the show. It was, for a time, during the 'twenties and 'thirties a considerable business, filling orders from Neiman Marcus, Marshall Field and Lord & Taylor as well as many individuals, among them Nazimova. And, although in the end, it did not withstand the depression, it helped put me through school, sent me to camp, and did indeed "help make ends meet" at a time when a considerable per cent of my father's income had to go to the support of my twin, *Isis.* But above all it satisfied my mother's need to "create" something of her own, to use her talents, and to find her own place in the new world. I still run into people now and then who bring out carefully preserved garments, faded from much use and laundering, on which the brilliant embroidered birds and flowers bear her signature.

The other unexpected gift had more lasting results. It was through my father's meeting with President Woodward of the Carnegie Institution that his long-held dream of writing the first complete history of science found support. President Woodward was interested, interested enough to offer the Institution's financial aid, believing enough to continue that help with no questions asked and no strings attached during the ten years or more of preliminary research before the first volume of *An Introduction to the History of Science* made its appearance. Under this generous arrangement my father could live and work where he pleased. At the same time L. J. Henderson of Harvard University invited the young scholar to give a lecture there, and shortly afterward suggested an arrangement by which George Sarton would give a half course at the University in exchange for a room in Widener Library. Thus our home in America was finally rooted in the city by the Charles, and there my parents lived until their deaths.

We were, as I look back on it now, unbelievably fortunate. And although my father never carried out his idea of a propaganda institute in Brussels, he never ceased to be grateful to this country; he had loved it from the beginning. There was some grain of truth in my child's vision of America, recognized first in the brown eyes of a Saint Bernard, in the kindness and natural wisdom of a chauffeur, in the imagination of a fairy godmother—an America whose breadth and dimension were suggested by the enormous robins and the fat tails of the squirrels. Later (not so very much later, in about ten years), I recognized it on another level when we, the graduating ninth grade at Shady Hill School got up gravely to recite, one by one, a stanza each of Walt Whitman's "Pioneers! O Pioneers!"

I had learned the poem by heart from our own copy of *Leaves of Grass*. A copy that had stayed in the house in Wondelgem all through the war was eventually brought over with the remains of my father's library, and has finally found a permanent place on my shelves in Cambridge. Just now, I took down this book and opened it. Had I never noticed the flyleaf before? I was astonished to find it inscribed, in my mother's hand, "George from Mabel, August 31st, 1910." They were not yet married. George Sarton had just received his Doctor's degree in celestial mechanics; Mabel Elwes was an art student, studying in Ghent. She could have had no idea how grave and prescient a gift it would turn out to be, but I, holding it now in my hands forty-eight years later, was moved to find there, on the flyleaf, one of those mysterious links in individual lives that can be seen only by going back in time.

I thought of Whitman's country—the physical country, to which we came so poor and hopeful, and which gave us so much—and of the great river that was my first image of America, and I thought also of the intangible Whitman country, the country of the dream. Would it be absurd to consider a small study in Widener Library at Harvard a province of that country, the study where George Sarton carried out his radical explorations into the past? Whitman's belief in a generous humanism that could encompass all mankind was really not so far from George Sarton's vision of the healing, unifying power of the history of science—not of one science but of all sciences, and not of one nation but of all nations from the beginning of time.

"George from Mabel, August 31st, 1910." And as Mabel Elwes chose this present for the man she was to marry, she an English girl, he a Belgian young man—a book of poems celebrating the New World—she was being carried forward without knowing it into a pattern that is now clearly visible. They were to become Americans, these two, and the foreign poet a compatriot. They were to have one child, who would find the book and the inscription after their deaths, and see in a flash the whole cycle of their lives, its apparent violent dislocations, its inner harmony—its beginning in a garden in Wondelgem, Belgium, its end a garden in Cambridge, Massachusetts, where my mother's English genius flowered, from the earliest snowdrop under the pine to the sequence of asters and chrysanthemums through November.

# II

## *The Education of a Poet*

*"In the fourth grade we were Greeks, a year I remember with particular happiness." May Sarton is kneeling, second from right*

## "I Knew a Phoenix in My Youth"

I was fortunate enough as a child to belong to the early days of the Shady Hill School, in Cambridge—the Co-operative Open Air School, as it was first called. It had been founded in 1915 by Agnes Hocking on the porch of her house, but by the time I went to it, in 1917, it had moved into buildings of its own, under the great willows near the Norton estate, Shady Hill, which gave it its final name. Here the school was really launched as one of the early "progressive" schools for boys and girls; here for the next eight years, punctuated only by two years spent abroad with my parents, I received my whole formal education until I entered the Cambridge High and Latin School for my last three years of high school. In those days, when Shady Hill was in every way in the making, we children must have seemed, as it were, a primitive insurgent tribe in the heart of conservative Cambridge. We had all the arrogance and some of the unsophisticated creativeness of such a tribe—filled with our own importance as part of a pioneering experiment, regarding other tribes as "lesser breeds without the Law." (I refer especially to those unfortunate girls who attended the Buckingham School, and those unfortunate boys who attended Browne and Nichols, both centrally heated.) A tribe we surely were, and primitive we must have seemed.

The buildings themselves were unorthodox. Built of wood and looking from the street side like low brown barracks, they were one large expanse of windows on the inner side facing the willows. These windows were kept open, even in zero weather. Only one room had a fireplace—the Big Room, where the school gathered each day for opening exercises. There was, it is true, a small potbellied wood stove at the teacher's end of each classroom, where frozen fingers might, in extremity, be painfully thawed, but this illusion of warmth made the polar regions at the back of the room seem even colder. We wrote in mittens, of course; as a result, some of us developed a hieroglyphic hand, today totally illegible even to ourselves, but fortunately the typewriter permits us to communicate. Our daily life in winter was rather like that of a team of mountain climbers on a lower alp, preparing for the final assault on an unknown peak. We dressed accordingly. This dress, which made one look like something between a bear and the Himalayan "Snowman," was to us as cherished a mark of distinction as the Eton boy's top hat generally is to him, though the effect may have been less impressive. Our costume began at the skin with long woolen underwear, and moved outward through layers of sweaters to the final apotheosis of a very long, heavy, gray sweater, buttoned down the front, which was bought deliberately, at Mrs. Hocking's suggestion, four sizes too large, so that it fell to the knees and actually became a coat. This successfully concealed dresses or knickerbockers, and was, in fact, our "uniform." Below the sweater, and over several pairs of woolen socks, we wore dark brown felt boots known as "woodchoppers' socks"; over them sheepskin-lined soft leather boots; and over them, huge shiny black rubbers. Mittens or gloves, tied together on a long frayed string, hung down from the sweater sleeves and flapped when not in use. Most of these items were acquired through the school commissary, which ordered them at school-discount rates from Sears Roebuck. When actually working in a classroom, we were further enveloped in heavy gray cocoons—sleeping bags that came up over our shoulders.

At the end of each class period, we jumped up and down in these bags, or occasionally were allowed to get out of them and run once or twice around the buildings, to start the circulation again. At eleven we were served hot cocoa in mugs. Learning under these conditions made us indisposed toward competitive sports in later life; we had been taught to think even when wholly numbed, and as adults we preferred contemplation to climbing mountains. We early graduates tend as a group to sedentary occupations, content in the memories of a heroic childhood.

But if the school taught us to endure physical hardship and to consider it an honor, this was hardly in itself an education. It may have cured me of a tendency to bronchitis and strengthened many a weak chest, but what more? Why did we believe in our inalienable right to feel like djinn bursting with mysterious power? There is no doubt that this creative state of mind stemmed in those early years from the genius of Agnes Hocking, the school's founder and moving spirit.

Mrs. Hocking was the wife of the philosopher, William Ernest Hocking, and the daughter of the poet, John Boyle O'Reilly; revolutionary blood flowed in her veins. The school was born of this marriage of poetry and philosophy, and though philosophy was worshiped, poetry ruled. Mrs Hocking never referred to her husband otherwise than as "Ernest Hocking," and always with the same intonation, which suggested that she considered him a deity. Once, discovering in the subway station at Harvard Square that she had forgotten her purse, she walked right past the collector, uttering the magic words "Ernest Hocking will give you five cents tomorrow" and sailed through the wicket.

As children in her school, we were caught up in a spiritual climate as bracing, as rich and unpredictable, as that of New England itself. We were not subjected to a theory of education. We were set down in the center of a primal force at work. We never knew what would happen next, but what did happen was always immensely interesting. We might, for instance, suddenly be punished—all sent to Coventry because one small person had fallen down and sprained an ankle. There was no logic in this meting out of judgment, but we thrived on it as did the Greeks on the changeable moods of Pallas Athene. It made us both stoical and imaginative. Mrs. Hocking was poetry incarnate. Her very person, glorious in red velvet on a special occasion, but more often resembling the old woman who lived in a shoe, was exhilarating. Soft wings of hair covered her brow; under them deep-set gray eyes twinkled, wept, or burned. She had small, quick hands, full of sudden caresses. I believe that she flew rather than walked.

She did not administer, she created, and part of the creation was, of course, to find teachers who would go their own way, unadministered. The word "co-operative" in the school's early name was as literal as the word "open-air." Shady Hill was founded to give the children of professors an ideal school, which the parents would invent and run themselves, and which would be within their limited means. There was no money to speak of; there were many scholarships. The excellent staff was made possible by the parents' pooling their skills, as teachers, as business managers, as secretaries, as helpers of all kinds, just as Henry Copley Greene became the official lighter of school plays, and Mr. Helburn, the official trainer in rock-climbing, who took groups of us off on Saturday afternoons to explore the rock-cliffs in the neighborhood of Cambridge. My mother taught applied design at Shady Hill for years, as she did later at the Winsor School. She believed that children, like primitive peoples, would enjoy making variations on simple geometric themes and applying these designs to useful and beautiful objects. What brilliant results emerged in this way from a design painted on a round ice-cream carton or wooden chopping bowl! The results had style and form, two elements that modern theories of "free painting" have apparently ceased to consider important. But I believe that children long for form just as grownups do, and that it releases rather than cramps creative energy. I was interested to rediscover the other day the original brochure advertising the school and to note that its aims were defined as: "To keep childhood alive to open-mindedness and a love of learning; to provide life with all possible richness and fullness; to secure freedom *with* self-control." *With* is underlined in the printed text, and one of the strengths of Shady Hill through the years, and long after Mrs. Hocking's retirement, was that that significant preposition was not forgotten. As I look back over the years that I spent in the school, I am very much aware that the emphasis on creativity and spontaneous expression was always balanced by a sense of the responsibility of each child toward the community, and above all respect not only for talent in each other, but for the ethical qualities summed up in the word "citizenship."

Ernest Hocking, in the early days of the school, helped keep this balance. When some crisis arose, it was he who descended, as it were, from Olympus, to tell us a short parable, as we "gathered together to ask the Lord's blessing" and sat on the low wooden benches unusually gravely, mesmerized by that serene smiling presence. Once an outbreak of anarchy rocked the school when a boy and girl from the twelfth grade got into a furious argument and tore up, to use for ammunition, a huge plasticine relief map of Europe that the smaller children had made. After the crime, the atmosphere of the whole school was funereal for several days, and finally Ernest Hocking, ineffably pink and serene, quietly glowing, drew us gently up from Hell by telling us a short but harrowing tale of two doves who destroyed their nest. I remember the relief with which we, the whole school, watched the two culprits stand, red to the ears, and solemnly shake hands. It seemed beautiful and good beyond words that there was a saving grace after all, and we never forgot the bliss of mutual forgiveness as we witnessed it that day.

We were a small, intense community, and all such affairs went deep. Sometimes the "co-operative" parents were the root of the trouble: in 1918 or thereabouts, when we were still singing the Marseillaise almost every morning, when feeling about the war ran high, and an owner of a dachshund in Boston had been attacked on the street as pro-German, they gathered together to protest the production of a play based on the Hansel and Gretel story. In the face of what seemed like a united front my mother rose up and spoke passionately to the point that if we allowed ourselves to indulge in such obtuse hatred that we could no longer see and accept the beautiful things Germany had given us, the Germans would in effect have won the war. This story was told me many years later by one of the parents—my mother herself had forgotten all about it.

Not all parents had the skill or the time to give, and there were from the beginning several professional teachers. In those early days, two women who are now legends to many generations of children came to the school, Miss Putnam and Miss Edgett. They were as different as night and day—two poles between whom we veered from excitement to calm. Miss Edgett taught mathematics. In her class, a mistake was not a private matter; it was wanton disturbance of the order of the universe. If I ever acquired a sense of sin, Miss Edgett conveyed it to me via a misplaced decimal point. She scrutinized our messy papers with great seriousness, as if they were matters of conscience rather than knowledge. An error of mine might be greeted with the *cri de guerre*, "May!

Your decimal point!" Then a rush to the blackboard, where, breaking a dozen pieces of chalk in her fury, Miss Edgett would whirl out a decimal point from a small button to an immense accusing sun.

I'm afraid we sometimes laughed; passion is always disturbing and we were young barbarians still. Sent out of the room, one could hear from afar the drama proceed. There might be some consolation in an apple produced from Mr. Lane's pocket—Mr. Lane was our beloved janitor—but one sat alone by the dying fire in the empty Big Room and felt sufficiently lonely; and one did mind not knowing what was going on. Perhaps in one's absence Miss Edgett would have given the accolade to a perfect paper. When she did, the whole class reflected her glow and we knew that though we were sinful, there was a mathematical Heaven within reach. For Miss Edgett not only loved mathematics, she loved us, and fitted us somehow into her universe, perhaps by means of an imagination that transcended her subject and permitted her to say about one not very talented mathematician, "May has a clear vision of the joy of numbers," a consummation arrived at through what patience and struggle on her part! For like every great teacher she taught more than her subject, and she helped teach me to be a poet:

> Only now later, it is clear how much
> Beyond exact and honored certainty
> You taught us then of deeper mystery:
> Poets begin with reverence for Truth.

I can see her—round, enthusiastic, quick—running out to sober us down as we filed along the boardwalk to opening exercises, and pouring fire on the troubled oil, so to speak, by shouting, "Keep down your nervous energy!"

Miss Putnam, on the other hand, lived in and created the kind of temperate climate in which plants, animals and children grow without knowing it. How was it that we always came into her room—the science room —as if on tiptoe, and silently? She never raised her voice, and neither did we, who shouted in every other class, a fact noted on my report card in Class 5 when my "General spirit" was called "good, but a voice ever soft gentle and low is an excellent thing in woman" (!) Miss Putnam's magic was to transform the primitive tribe into a group of serious scientists in pursuit of the truth. We were a little afraid of her. She did not bother to praise or blame, since both praise and blame were irrelevant to the matter at hand, which might be the phases of the moon, or the growth of a frog from the eggs we had gathered ourselves from a nearby pond, to the living frog we had also brought back in a glass jar. There were, as I remember, no textbooks at all. We made our own, through our own observations, and the slow patient Socratic process of Miss Putnam's questions to us. She respected in us the impersonal qualities—the ability to be detached, to wait, to be precise—and we had to rise to that respect. She never told us anything, but she led us very quietly, almost casually, to the point where we might find it out for ourselves, or find it out together as a team in which, perhaps, the imagination of one child would be balanced by the cautious realism of another. As the years went on, we lost our constraint and came to love her. I remember, one year, tracing off with great care a map of the world in the shape of a heart to give her as a valentine; I never did dare tell her that it was I who had made the map. But how I longed to!

We had also weekly visitations from Mrs. Neal, who unfolded from rolls of linen the flat, limp bodies of birds, so brilliant, so soft, that their beauty was alarming. These we could touch, opening the wings or tail feathers to see the structure, stroking the soft breasts, disturbed a little by the tight-closed eyes and still claws. On Saturday mornings, some of us gathered at dawn, to go out with Mrs. Neal into the country and look for the living members of each species. How thrilling it was to get up before daylight, when the whole world was asleep, and bicycle through the empty streets, past the closed houses, to this early-morning gathering! Sometimes our walk across stubbly fields and through brambles was rewarded—once, I remember, by the glorious sight of six bluebirds on a sumac tree.

There was the great year when one part of the primitive tribe reached the fourth grade and was metamorphosed into civilized Greeks, under the direction of Mary Hotson, the wife of the Elizabethan scholar Leslie Hotson, for as we progressed through the school we progressed through history: we had been Indians in the third grade; we would be Romans in the fifth, and not become Americans until the eighth, after passing through the "Age of Exploration and Discovery" in the seventh. Meanwhile in the fourth grade we were Greeks, a year I remember with particular happiness. We stenciled white sheets and made them into chitons, spent happy hours carving the Acropolis out of Ivory soap, learned Greek songs (notably a prayer to Athene which

[ *110* ]

still haunts me), and made private oblations to our chosen gods. These joys were marred only by my entire failure to master the art of punctuation, so that my themes came back with thunderous exclamation points in red pencil, a perpetual cross. But that was a minor matter compared to entering and becoming part of the world of mythology. One day, two of us were inspired to kneel down close to the Harvard Divinity School, whose grounds we traversed on our way home, and stop a passer-by, intoning the proper incantations to inform him that he would have sixty children and that from the mouths of thirty of them frogs would be spewed out and from the mouths of the other thirty, pieces of gold. Our passer-by entered into the spirit of the thing and seemed properly delighted at this prospect. The climax of the year was the production of a Greek play, but, alas, I do not remember what it was—nor will they come again, "the long, long dances."

This was all very well, and in fact magnificent teaching, but it was not the very core of the school under Agnes Hocking. For the core of the school and its unique strength lay in the one fact that here poetry was made centrally active. Agnes Hocking taught this subject—if what she did can be called by any such formal name as teaching—to the whole school. She did it all day long, by bursting into spontaneous prayer when the spirit moved her, by those sudden noble angers, and, more formally, by meeting with each class for a scheduled hour. No doubt there was method, but to us it was heavenly madness, was delight—the opening of a door into a land where everything on earth seemed gathered together and harmonized. It was, on the whole, a noisy

school. But I have seen Agnes Hocking, sitting on a
low chair before the open fire in the Big Room, create
such stillness in a hundred or more boys and girls of all
ages that they themselves quite clearly heard the silence
above the noise of a passing trolley and the crackle of
the fire. She did not tell us about poetry; she made us
live its life. This creation of stillness, for instance, was
the introduction to a little poem by Edward Rowland
Sill called "Peace." One or another of us might be called
on to say it, or we might say it together, or she might
say it. But no one spoke until there was perfect silence,
until all of us together had sat with our eyes shut for
perhaps two minutes, and when the final line was spoken,
"Peace is here," no one moved for ages and ages; peace
*was* there. This was a fairly complex delight for small
children. She also gave us simpler ones. Sometimes we all
became seals, a thing rather easy to do if you are already
sitting in a gray woolen bag. We simply lay down on
our backs on the floor, while the Big Room became an
ocean, and murmured:

> "Where billow meets billow, there soft be thy
>     pillow;
> Ah, weary wee flipperling, curl at thy ease!
> The storm shall not wake thee, nor shark
>     overtake thee,
> Asleep in the arms of the slow-swinging seas."

The floor swayed slightly below us and we rolled
over. Mrs. Hocking, also in a gray bag on the floor, was
the Seal of Seals.

Even purely technical matters became magic. Once
she turned on me in apparent fury and shouted "You

goose!" and then, before I had time to burst into tears, added in an explanatory tone, "That's a metaphor." I never had to be told in so many words that metaphor explodes and simile is pale beside it. "You goose! That's a metaphor" had made it abundantly clear.

We were not given a poem to read or study; we learned each one through hearing it repeated by Mrs. Hocking until we knew it by heart. Knew it by heart? We had become whatever it was long before we guessed we were learning it. We learned poems by osmosis—the only good way, I am convinced. Our memory of the words was a reflex action that accompanied certain gestures—for instance, making the long ears of a hare when we repeated Walter de la Mare's "Witch Hare." Even now I find it embarrassing to recite this poem because I can't keep my hands at my sides; they wish to become ears. Alain, the philosopher, speaks somewhere of poetry as "a kind of music which is physiologically right." Therein lay its excitement for us. It was not something told, it was something happening to us all the time. On warm spring days, we moved outside to sit on benches under a large red maple. There, one day, we discovered that Sir William Watson's poem about April, for all its sentimental diction, was absolutely real. In the very middle of our reciting:

> "April, April,
>   Laugh thy girlish laughter;
>   Then, the moment after,
>   Weep thy girlish tears!"

a shower fell upon us and drove us in, suffused with laughter—in this case, the laughter of recognition. Did

Agnes Hocking summon that cloud herself, I wonder. It would not have surprised us at all if she had.

So it was really not strange, considering all this, that when President Eliot of Harvard, an old man then and long retired, met a Shady Hill child on the street—a child unknown to him but wearing the mark of the primitive tribe (those sheepskin boots, that incredibly long gray sweater)—and asked, "Where do you go to school?" and the child answered, "To the best school in the world," the shy old man smiled and said, "Shady Hill, I presume?"

By the time I reached the fifth grade, Mrs. Hocking had retired as active head, though she still taught poetry. For an interim period the school was becalmed while efforts were made to discover the genius—nothing less would have been adequate—who could take the helm in her place. And in Katharine Taylor, from the Parker School in Chicago, this genius was found. I remember very well the mixture of curiosity and chauvinism with which we observed our new "head," for we had suffered under the absence rather than the presence of her predecessor, a distinguished historian, but too frail to withstand the duties of commanding a primitive tribe. We were not to be easily convinced. I suppose we felt obscurely that the school was "ours" and that any new element which came in would come as an invader and to "change" us in some unforeseeable direction. So Katharine Taylor, tall, slim, acutely sensitive, swift in her response, took on a formidable task. I remember her in those days as observing us with a mixture of intense concern and mirth; what we observed in her, what soon commanded our devotion, was the quite necessary quality of poetry personified. Nothing less could have won the day.

She brought to the school with her another of the great teachers who made Shady Hill what it was, Anne Thorp, who, a granddaughter of Longfellow, was returning to home base. It is not my purpose here to assess what was happening; I can only relate its effect at the time. But I suppose I could say that in the last four years at Shady Hill I completed as much formal education as I would have. There has been so much misapprehension about what we were taught, about the kinds of permissiveness, about the standards of so-called "progressive" schools, that I feel compelled to speak in some detail about these final formative years, and what, as I look back, I learned. First of all the school was then, and has remained, primarily a congregation of extraordinary teachers, as different from each other in method and approach as it is possible to imagine, as different from each other in temperament as are the planets. Where the directing genius of Katharine Taylor was made manifest was in the continual balanced emphasis between the social responsibility of each one of us and his individual development. On the one hand we had reverence for each other's talents: I remember the excitement with which I ran home one day to announce to my mother, "Peter Sprague is a genius!" Until then Peter and I had simply been good friends, our friendship cemented so to speak in the blood of mice, for we had made a mouse cemetery in his backyard, and spent a good deal of time ringing doorbells and asking people if they had any dead mice we could bury. But on the day in question he had created a musical instrument out of a small crate and some wires of different lengths and strengths strung across it. I was awed. This was the real thing, and I had been often shown at school that my own quickness and desire to excel in everything, was often not the "real" thing.

We were brought up certainly to be individuals, but we were constantly made aware of our relationship to each other, and taught to respect and cherish differences. The great experiences of the school were those we created out of our several skills and shared together. I am thinking of the Christmas play, of the very remarkable music—the yearly performance of Brahms' Requiem, for example—or of the gradual unfolding of understanding of a scientific phenomenon in one of Miss Putnam's classes.

Plays were as much a part of our daily lives at school as was poetry and the saying of poems, and the first overwhelming gift I remember Katharine Taylor making, was the creation of a Christmas play using parts of Isaiah, to lead up to the New Testament Nativity scene. This play is rooted in the being of those of us who participated in it through the years. There was nothing "progressive" about the long hours we spent working to make our diction worthy of the great words, nor was there anything childish about the play itself. Henry Copley Greene, a parent at that time, designed a set of large gray boxes, heavy crates, really, that could be shifted about to make mountains, a temple, or whatever the play of the moment required.

But in my mind's eye this set of boxes is always standing in a dim light while two children, dressed in somber colors and representing "Man" and "Woman" recite antiphonally:

"Behold, the Lord maketh the earth empty. All joy is darkened, the mirth of the land is gone."

"Jehovah hath forsaken me, and the Lord hath forgotten me."

"How shall I comfort thee? It is a day of perplexity; a breaking down of the walls, and a crying to the mountains."

"We grope for the wall like the blind; we look for light, but behold darkness."

And then, as Henry Copley Greene brought on the dawn, Woman turned to the two Watchmen standing on their gray box towers and said:

"Watchman, what of the night?"

"The morning cometh."

And the Second Watchman pointed down through the assembled children and parents to Mary Dewing, wrapped in a white cashmere shawl, who would come through us as the Prophet of the Messiah, and speak the haunting words: "How beautiful upon the mountains are the feet of him that bringeth good tidings, that publisheth peace." It was one of the great moments of our lives.

The plays were sometimes our own creation, even to the words. Under Mrs. Reynolds in first-year Latin, we wrote and acted a play in Latin about a Roman school, not only wrote and acted but made costumes for it, and learned to feel like young Romans by becoming them.

We were given much; we took much for granted. As I look back now on the great year of medieval history we spent with Anne Thorp in Grade VII, I realize what work went into the constant use of source materials, the lack of a textbook, which meant that everything we learned was alive, hunted down, a private possession, but meant in our teachers a devotion and eagerness for work that seems little short of miraculous. We were taught thoroughness, respect for sources, taught how to find out what we needed to know by ourselves, learned young to use encyclopedias and reference books, and to have a certain healthy contempt for any information that did not come "from the horse's mouth." Above all we were taught to think, and to respect solid good work. Standards of performance were to some extent graded in accordance with a child's capacity, but standards of effort, of work itself, were high. They could be maintained because school was the element in which we felt most at home, like fish in water. We lived and breathed the school; we felt we were creating it just as concretely as it was creating us. So I remember going to Katharine Taylor in the ninth grade and demanding to have more poetry, as a right. Did she yield some Aristotle to the poets? I do not remember. But the point is that it was the kind of school where the students were actively involved to the limit of their energies, and sometimes a little beyond. Possibly I can suggest the kind of fervor we felt and the kind of attention we were given, by quoting some passages from a letter Miss Putnam wrote the mother of a member of my class:

"I do appreciate the work and spirit which your daughter brings to me. I have never taught a keener mind or a more thoroughly conscientious spirit. I think if anything she passes the peak of efficiency and slips over on the other side by working too long and thinking too intensely. We ought to help her to take life a little less seriously. . . . She cares so much in a test or a speech, that she does not always reach the highest level. . . . If she continually works too long, won't you just put a stop to it, tell her it is by my own request, that I want to see just how much can be done in a given period? If all my pupils were of this type, I need never assign any home lessons, but some of them need to be kept busy on something concrete like a paper or a drawing in order to train either their minds or their morals."

I have copied this passage because I trust it will help explode the myth that the "progressive" school is a sort of *laissez-aller* chaos where children yearn for discipline. At least, not so was Shady Hill.

Almost all of this is ancient history. The school is no longer "open-air." It has moved into larger grounds and new buildings at the other end of Cambridge. But until very recently Miss Edgett was still making huge decimal points on the blackboard; Miss Putnam was helping generations of boys and girls to be not only knowledgeable but humble and wise. Shady Hill is no doubt still to many a child the best school in the world. But we, the prehistoric ones, who remember Mrs. Hocking and the genius who succeeded her, will, I trust, be forgiven for secretly thinking, "I knew a phoenix in my youth, so let them have their day."

## A Belgian School

Nothing could have been more different from Shady Hill than the Institut Belge de Culture Française where I went to school for a winter when I was twelve. Twelve is not one of the easiest years in any child's life.

The Institut was a many-windowed, low brick house in the newer part of Uccle, a suburb of Brussels that still keeps its flavor of a village. There are open meadows with cows in them nearby, and a magnificent formal park, once a private estate, where one can walk through avenues of immense beech trees and on carpets of bronze leaves; there is a charming eighteenth-century church and market square. In spite of its formidable name, the school was anything but an institution in the usual meaning of that word.

Its faculty consisted entirely of two remarkable women. Its founder and presiding genius, Marie Closset, a friend of Gide and Francis Jammes, was well known in the world of Belgian and French letters as the poet Jean Dominique: my father had carried a volume of hers in his pocket in 1904, believing perhaps that the author was a young man, as did Charles Van Lerberghe,

*"Marie Closset, well-known as the poet Jean Dominique, was to become one of the two or three primary influences in my life."*

who wrote her a word of praise when her first book appeared, but remarked that the style was rather feminine. She had begun her teaching career at the Ecole Normale, in Brussels, but she had soon rebelled against both the method and the content of the teaching there. The Institut was the product of her imagination and will, built to her own design sometime after World War I, with the help of generous friends who believed in what she wanted to do and who wished their children to study in the kind of atmosphere she created. Marie Closset—who was later to become one of the two or three primary influences in my life—hardly impinged on my consciousness at first, for I was in the lower school, which was made up of boys and girls who were being prepared to take the examinations for the *athènée*, the Belgian equivalent of our high school, and she had given the teaching of "the little ones" over to her friend and disciple, Marie Gaspar.

These two lived in separate apartments on the second floor, that secret "upstairs" that we children wondered about and never saw. There was also a third member of the household—Blanche Rousseau, the novelist, who after her husband's death came to share her life with these two old friends. We saw her rarely—tiny, white-haired, with radiant blue eyes. The three ladies shared the cozy dining room and kitchen behind the classrooms, as well as the ministrations of an excellent cook. At the back of the house, there was a small orchard and garden, where the thrushes gathered each year to steal the cherries and where gala ceremonies took place on the last day of school, when "the little ones" were garlanded with flowers and hung with medals—chocolate medals, wrapped in gold foil.

A flagstone path bordered by hydrangeas led to the pretty, oval-corniced front door, where we pulled the bell each morning and heard it resound inside. Once in the hall, we hung up capes or coats on a stand and then turned left into the airy, sunny room that was our school. The room on the right-hand side of the hall was used mostly in the afternoons and was Marie Closset's domain. Here she taught older children, who came to her for special courses in art and literature; here also she gave teachers in the official Brussels schools, many of them former pupils of hers from the *Normale*, instruction and inspiration. Mlle. Closset was from the beginning "Cher Maître"; Marie Gaspar was known to the younger pupils as simply "Titi."

Titi was the same breed as Agnes Hocking, the founder of Shady Hill; Mrs. Hocking was half Irish, and the Irish and the Belgians have in common, it would seem, humor, temperament, and a love of language for its own sake. Titi might look and behave like a clown and a genius and the mother superior of a convent, all in the winking of an eye. She was almost never still—a small, angular figure with a face extremely fine and sensitive in repose. But it was seldom in repose. She had a piercing voice capable of every shade of irony, fury, passion, and tenderness. At Shady Hill, I had not been exposed to a personality of this voltage all day long, for we had had Agnes Hocking only at certain hours. But Titi taught us every subject, from mathematics and natural science to art and literature. We were never for a moment free from her intense interest and concern. At recess, she took us on nature walks; in study hour she sat with brilliant, snapping eyes, obviously reading our every thought.

My problems were rather special. Because my father had had to learn English when we came to America, we always spoke English at home. I understood French and could speak it more or less fluently, but my grammar was shaky, and therefore, since French was, of course, the school language, all my formal studies required an extra effort. The change from English weights and measures to the metric system further confused me. Problems that ran, "If you took a keg of cider and divided it by three and multiplied that third by a fourth, how many litres would you have?" induced in me incipient hysteria. The blood rushed to my head and I felt like an idiot.

I was transplanted not only from one system of weights and measures to another, and from one language to another, but from one theory of education to another, and this was the real trouble. At Shady Hill we had been taught to think for ourselves and would have been looked at askance had we memorized a text or recited word for word anything we had been given to learn. Here at the Institut Belge, under Mlle. Gaspar, memory was of the essence. We were expected to learn our textbooks quite literally by heart from cover to cover. The substitution of an equally accurate word for a word in the text would result in a black mark or a scream of horror from Titi. I cannot now look at a page of the French textbook of natural science that we used—a page on the anatomy of the rodent, for instance—without being seized by fear and trembling. The words "herbivore" and "carnivore" appear in my nightmares, and the very idea of the number of teeth in the lower jaw of a horse brings on panic.

My mother and I were living that winter with old friends in the country outside Brussels—Céline and Raymond Limbosch, who had played such important parts in George Sarton's and Mabel Elwes's lives in the fervent years before World War I. My mother had longed to get back to Europe for a time after the first hard years of adopting America and making new roots. My father, who had stayed in Cambridge to finish some work, was to join us there for the summer. The two older Limbosch children, Jacques and Claire, were roughly my age; we attended the Institut together. Every morning, Oncle Raymond, as I called him, spent fifteen exasperating minutes getting his ancient open automobile to start, while no one dared speak and we became more and more nervous that we might be late. Finally we all piled in—his wife ("Mamie" we all called her), my mother, Jacques, Claire and I—and, accompanied by a series of backfiring explosions and last-minute shouts to Bobo, the governess, we were off. We children were dropped at a corner about a mile from the school, and Oncle Raymond drove on with Mamie and my mother to L'Art Décoratif, the Limboschs' family business in town, for Céline had inherited her mother's business and moved it to Brussels, and my mother was again working for them as a designer, as she had done for Madame Dangotte in Ghent in the old days.

Never, never shall I forget the long descent of the Avenue de Fré toward the Institut each morning. Carrying our books in straps, wearing heavy gray capes and rubber boots (did it always rain that winter?), we took a look at Paradise, it seemed, as we passed and peered through the iron railings of an old estate at a mysterious pond full of duckweed and overshadowed by ancient chestnuts, where a single swan swam alone. I dreamed of climbing over somehow and escaping into that green place, never to be seen again. Instead we hurried, compelled by a fearful anxiety that made our hearts beat too fast: would Titi scold us today? Was some terrible storm brewing? Sometimes we stopped to take a last desperate look at the *Herbivores* and the *Carnivores* in our textbook, but more often we simply walked doggedly forward, tense and silent. It was the descent into Hell. Never for a single day during that winter did I know the luxury of being well prepared. The last glimpse of Heaven was the cows (how I envied them!) in the big sloping meadow near the Ferme Rose, an old pink farm that is still a landmark in Uccle.

Pale with anxiety, we turned into the Avenue de l'Echevinage just below the farm. I sometimes wonder what it was, exactly, that induced such panic even in the Limbosch children, who were at home in the French language and methods of instruction. Perhaps it had to do with Marie Gaspar's nature. She was so very sudden, so quick herself in all her responses, that we always felt we were breathlessly trying to catch up. Her pouncing rages were so terrifying that we could never feel safe. Also, she had, I see now, a very innocent mind. She had absorbed, exactly in the way she expected us to absorb it—word for word—everything Marie Closset had taught her, and she did not have enough confidence in herself to be willing to allow us to deviate. Actually, the courses, supervised by Marie Closset, were rich and various, and much of the material we were given was splendid. But the lower school had to meet the requirements of the rigid *athènée* exams, and here Marie Gaspar depended on memorizing—perhaps, again, because she was not entirely sure of herself. She did din the facts into our heads, and could always point to her success from the examiner's point of view if anyone questioned her rather rigid demands. I have an idea that at some point Marie Closset realized that this was not quite the school she dreamed of, and suffered. But by then Mlle. Gaspar was firmly entrenched, immensely successful—and what was one to do? Marie Closset knew very well that though Titi was feared, she was also adored. And once we children got to school, the actual experience of the classroom was rarely as awful as we imagined it would be, for Titi could be as easily carried away by delight at any sign of intelligence as by fury at stupidity or forgetfulness. Also, she had a saving grace—a fantastic original sense of humor, Belgian in its extravagance, bordering on the grotesque, which often broke the tension with a storm of laughter. While she wiped her eyes and we had trouble keeping ourselves straight up on the benches, the cramped and cramping fears vanished; we were set free. Besides, she loved each of us with a passionate and discriminating love, and we knew it. And if, at the end of the day, a child was reduced to tears, the effect was instantaneous. The fiery eyes softened; she came around behind the long benches on which we sat, in front of long tables covered with black oilcloth, and comforted the unhappy one with kisses or told him an irresistible joke of her own invention. I'm afraid I cried rather often.

I was, after all, twelve, and probably at that age

a less electric atmosphere would have been to the point. I was upsetting myself enough without being further troubled by someone outside. Raymond Limbosch, the father of Claire and Jacques, was a poet as well as a designer, at that time, of exquisite modern furniture for his wife's firm; he was also, and always would be, a philosopher at heart, hunting like an ancient alchemist for the philosophers' stone. Sometimes this curiosity led him astray. And, unfortunately, during that winter of 1924–25, he was fascinated by an amateur psychologist—my father later called him a quack—who believed that he could read character traits by examining the eyes of the subject closely. We children were, each in turn, examined by this man, who must indeed have been a quack, and an insensitive one at that, since he pronounced his verdict in front of the child he had examined. He predicted that I would become a lawyer or a dancer. It was not too remote a guess, for I did have dreams of becoming a dancer at that time and I did love controversy. I used to carry on a running battle with the Limbosch family about the superiority of America (as I called it then—never the United States) over any other country, past or present. I tried their patience by singing "America the Beautiful" in a loud tuneless contralto. It was, I am sure, irritating, but it was also exhausting to me, since the Limbosch children of my age outnumbered me by two to one, and even the little ones baited me by screaming "America! America!" I was argumentative but also very suggestible and, unluckily the good doctor had said, further, that I had a very small brain, which I worked dangerously hard. I was deeply offended and frightened by his diagnosis, and the fright took the form of a waking nightmare. I imagined that I carried around, instead of a brain, a small, very active spider which was eating me up. With this image in my consciousness all the time, it became harder and harder for me to concentrate. Any intellectual effort brought the blood to my head, and for a time I was convinced that I was going mad. Of course, the grownups soon became aware of this delusion, and everything possible was done to counteract the doctor's words. But words are more powerful than perhaps anyone suspects, and, once deeply engraved in a child's mind, they are not easily eradicated.

Then, little by little, I began to discover that in one subject, at least, I could hold my own. We were given a great deal of literature, both prose and poetry, to learn by heart, or to take down in *dictées*. We were also expected to write short *rédactions*—chiefly descriptions of places and people, in which style and mood were carefully analysed in the French manner. Here, where feeling and expression counted more than grammar, I learned that, far from being blocked by the strange language, I could take positive delight in using it.

It now becomes necessary to say a word about the other half of the school, for as I began to enjoy French composition, I gradually became aware that there was another, and even more powerful presence involved— Marie Closset herself. As in our room, hers, across the hall, had on the walls reproductions of paintings beginning with Fra Angelico and going on down to the Impressionists, many of whom she had known; as in ours, there were shelves of books, and long tables and benches. Otherwise, it was a wholly different world. Our world was noisy with laughter and tribulation; hers was so inward, so still, so infused with her remarkable personality, that it created an atmosphere of awe.

She was herself a tiny figure, rather stooped and diminished by constant ill health; this frail aspect served perhaps to exaggerate her enormous luminous gray eyes behind dark glasses, which she put on and took off with a rhythmical gesture as she read or spoke. It was not a beautiful face in any ordinary sense, but it was a face so filled by the spirit and the intellect, so transparent to its own inwardness, that it was memorable. She had small hands with the lightness and grace of wings, and a grave, quietly expressive voice made for the reading of poetry. No wonder she hid those amazing eyes; they were too revealing. Genius in its purest form—love—looked out of them.

She taught literature almost entirely by reading from great works and commenting upon them, and these ranged from Plato and Aristotle to Tolstoy and the moderns of all nations. She also gave a course in Japanese Art, a course in Renaissance Art, a course in Greek Art, and many more; in fact, she chose to teach what moved her deeply, and nothing else. Later on, when I was grown up, I attended some of these classes as a listener, and I never heard her say a disparaging word about a work of art. What she wished to instill in her students was enlightened homage—homage enriched by intellectual analysis but rooted in passion. To professors of literature in our American colleges, this may seem a startling way to teach, for here it has become the fashion to analyze works of art before they have been deeply experienced by the students—a method that may, at its worst, engender in the young a sense of slightly smug superiority to the naïveté and flaws of genius. Marie Closset's attitude, on the other hand, was perfectly expressed in her demand that her students rise when she came in, not to honor her but to honor what they were about to hear or see—those bundles of notebooks and portfolios she brought down from the magic "upstairs," and herself so reverently opened.

I have tried to convey the atmosphere of the room across the hall as I came to know it many years later. But when I was twelve, Marie Closset first appeared to me through her handwriting. When a student of Marie Gaspar's wrote something she felt was worthy of the master's attention, this attention was given, as the highest reward possible, in the form of a few lines written on the paper in that round, clear, luminous hand. Her comment might be simply, *"Bien senti!"* (Can you imagine such a phrase on the paper of a high-school student in America today? Not "Watch your dependent clauses" but "This is truly felt.") During that strange winter of crisis, she was a distant balm, an angel whom I hardly ever saw but whose presence in the house made life bearable for me.

My experience at the Institut was not by any means a wholly negative one. I suffered, but I learned a good deal, too—learned to respect the memory, even though I would never possess a very good one, and learned to respect the exact, instead of the almost exact, word. Also, Titi, in spite of her tantrums, was enormous fun, and a year was not really too long for a child to be swung about at random under that rich and violent temperament. She had the ability to make us feel that we were not only her pupils, but her dearest friends as well, and I believe that this was a fact. Unlike Marie Closset, who had an intense life of her own apart from the school, Titi literally lived in and for her pupils.

And we cannot, after all, have been so afraid of her, for on April Fool's Day she was the butt of many jokes, one of which, organized by the older students, has become a kind of legend. Unfortunately, I have to rely on reports of this, because I had been sick and was away at the seaside when it happened. It seems that ten days before April first the unsuspecting Titi received a letter postmarked Ghent and announcing that her cousin Marie-Virginie (who gave no family name) planned to visit her "dear cousin Marie" very soon, accompanied by her four daughters. Titi, horrified, tried vainly to remember whether there was a cousin Marie-Virginie in the family. She wrote her brother to inquire whether he had any idea who this cousin might be. She dispatched another letter to her sister in Arlon, but even this sister, who was an expert on all family matters, had never heard of a Marie-Virginie in Ghent. Meanwhile, since Titi heard no more, she began to feel reassured. But a few days later a second letter, still bearing no family name, created a state of panic. The cousin wrote, "At last everything is arranged. I shall arrive in Brussels with my four daughters to pay you a visit a week from Wednesday. We shall talk, alas, about my difficult situation." One can imagine the laughter and terror with which this letter was discussed "upstairs" by the three friends. It was an event in anyone's life—it became so in mine when I was grown up—to be invited for tea or a meal into the magic circle created by three tiny, brilliant women who were interested in almost everything under the sun and who could be both extremely serious and extremely gay. As each of the three, in her way, was much loved and sought after, social invitations—how to fit them in—became a real problem for them. And callers or visiting relatives, especially distant relatives, had the effect of an interruption to a piece of music, a trio by Mozart. Titi, thoroughly alarmed by the second letter, and dreading a request for money from a cousin she did not know existed, wrote by return mail to "Madame" at the address given, to say that she could not receive anyone on the date suggested and that she would be grateful if Marie-Virginie would tell her family name. Meanwhile, the mother of Livia, one of the conspirators, asked for an appointment with Titi after class on the fateful Wednesday, April first, to make sure that she would be at home. So when Wednesday afternoon came, the three friends were waiting innocently upstairs for Livia's mother. The bell rang at a quarter to five. The cook opened the door, gave the formidable matron and her four daughters one startled look, ran up the stairs bearing a visiting card, and handed it to Titi. Giving a cry of despair, she said, "It's the other one."

"What other?" Marie Closset, who was absorbed in a book, asked abstractedly.

"The famous Marie-Virginie, of course. What ever shall I do?" And with that Titi ran down.

As soon as she made her appearance in the hall, the huge matron (Livia, disguised by pillows, a large hat and a long black veil, and by an old-fashioned coat with a high fur collar) rushed toward her to give her the ritualistic Belgian kiss, one on each cheek, and one more for good measure, saying, in a cloyingly sweet voice, "Here we are, dear Cousin Marie—at last!" The four "daughters" stood, as straight as ramrods, in front of the hall bench. Livia tried to go on, but the bread she had stuffed into her mouth to disguise her voice melted at this moment, and suddenly Titi caught on, recognized her, and gave a shriek of delight and amazement. It was not hard now to make out the familiar faces of Denise, Antoinette, Nanette and Nellie, in spite of their grotesque assemblage of borrowed coats and cloche hats, their noses made up bright red, and large paper parcels of the *spécialités de Gand*, such as *pain à la grecque*, clutched in their hands. The two upstairs heard shrieks of laughter and came down to join in the fun.

That evening, Titi continued the joke on her own by making her brother think that the unknown cousin really existed and had borrowed money from her, leading him on until he got quite furious, and was about to make a scene. And then the tale had to be told all over again.

If this occasion is indelibly clear in my mind, it is because I have in my possession a painting representing it, which was sent to me in triumph by one of the conspirators, and also because I have heard the story so often that I have almost come to believe that I was present myself—that I was, in fact, one of the mythical daughters and, with the others, sat down to that wonderful tea in the dear old dining room, its wall hung with blue delft plates, its copper jugs gleaming on the sideboard.

It does not seem possible that that room has now been dismantled, and that there are no more rubber boots and capes on the stand in the hall, no more loud cries and shouts of laughter in the brick house, but only a bronze plaque (so I am told) to commemorate the fact that here lived the poet Jean Dominique, the novelist Blanche Rousseau. The plaque makes no mention of that violent and tender teacher, Marie Gaspar. And this is just, perhaps. Teachers live on in human lives, not in books. Besides, Marie Gaspar is celebrated in one of the last works of Jean Dominique, a memoir that appeared in the Belgian review *Le Thyrse*, written to do her friend homage. I translate from a passage in the middle:

"Your dear absent-minded laugh, sonorous, a bit mad, was one of the charms of this house that sheltered so simply and so graciously three old ladies moving toward death. . . . Naturally, though no one would have thought of mentioning it, it seemed certain that of these three, the eldest, who, besides, was sickly, would be the first to go. And as for the youngest, more cherished than the others because she was more exquisite, no one could imagine her death, for the simple reason that she loved life with such a passionate and charming love that one often had the impression, even in her simplest act, as she said good morning or good night, that she was blowing a kiss to everything that exists. . . .

"For you, Gaspari, one must go back to what Francis de Miomandre . . . said with so much heart and spirit. What was it? Just this, in answer to my letter telling of your death: 'It's not true. Gaspari is not dead, and I know that she is immortal. . . .'

"I think of one day when she came back from taking her turbulent troop out on a spring walk. Everything felt so deliciously free that the cries of the children as they ran madly about seemed as marvelously fugitive as the words of the hawthorn, swallow, and buzzing bee. And this is what happened in that immortal minute: Gaspari had that day, as usual, punished one of the children for not having done his homework, and the punishment consisted of his not being allowed to run about freely with the other children, intoxicated as they were by their pleasure. But she had said to the punished one, 'You will go out with us, but you cannot play. You can only walk quietly beside me, and I will hold your hand.' Ah, Gaspari, what a good idea that was, and what a charming smile you bent toward the child, who felt himself so wonderfully punished and forgiven, so cross and so happy, even glorious, because he could hold your hand! And from the child's small hand something unexpected flowed out: the supreme contentment of understanding and love, a thing immortal in fact, which lasts only a moment and which one never forgets."

## "The High and Latin"

I graduated from Shady Hill in 1926, feeling that my education had been accomplished, though to a grown-up mind it would appear scarcely to have begun. Shady Hill went only through the ninth grade, the equivalent of first year high school; at that point our class of twelve was divided into those who went on to a private school and a small flying wedge of us who chose instead the formidable, the democratic, the highly populated "High and Latin," the Cambridge public high school. Entering in the second year, we missed all initiating experiences; we were catapulted from a small intimate group into a class of three hundred, into a "home room" from which we emerged to run down interminable corridors to other rooms where our subjects—Latin, English, French, Geometry, Chemistry—were taught over the years. We moved in and out of classes of sixty boys and girls, many of whose names we never knew.

At Shady Hill we had participated intensely in the life around us; the school, indeed, appeared to *be* life, and, emerging therefore old in experience (or so we believed), we regarded further formal studies with scepti-

*"...graduation...the end of my formal education..."*

cism, convinced that our education might better take place anywhere but in school. Luckily for ourselves and our teachers, we were interested in so many things that our entire energy could not be used up in rebellion inside the huge yellow brick building where we gathered reluctantly every morning. A good part of it was absorbed in the first months in preparing a production of *Peter Pan* which we presented as a farewell performance from our class to the Shady Hill community: we were not really quite weaned, and it was a way of making roots in the new Shady Hill, for the year after our graduation, the buildings around the old willows were abandoned and a new school rose on Coolidge Hill. The new Big Room seemed vast indeed; but fortunately it provided a balcony from which Peter Pan could fly down to the gray boxes (they at least, unchanged from what they were, though considerably battered). We were actors and writers, rather than students at this time. Did we really spend hours in the Harvard Co-op smelling the different leathers of the expensive notebooks we felt necessary as binding for anthologies of our favorite poems by Francis Thompson, Edna St. Vincent Millay, H. D. and Carl Sandburg? I seem to remember that we did. Several notebooks were needed, for we were poets ourselves, of course, and collected our own and each other's works, carefully copied out in illegible hands. I had two intimate friends at this time, Jean Tatlock and Letty Field. We met after school to go on long expeditions up the Charles River, still lined in willows then, still open country back of Mt. Auburn Cemetery. We walked, reciting Francis Thompson's "Hound of Heaven" in chorus, or engaged in fierce arguments or simple exclamations of communion over Rosamond Lehman's *Dusty Answer*, Isadora Duncan's *Autobiography*, the League of Nations, or the Sacco-Vanzetti case. Woodrow Wilson was our hero. We went to the theatre in twenty-five cent seats (!) in the last row of the balcony at the Boston Repertory to see *Hedda Gabler, Macbeth,* and *Quality Street,* and haunted the stage door for a glimpse of our star, Katharine Warren. We went three nights in succession to Fritz Leiber's *Hamlet,* transported by our first experience of a play that we proceeded to learn by heart. We went to the Boston Symphony concerts at Sanders Theatre on standing-room tickets, and, as soon as the lights were dimmed, lay on the floor behind the high wooden backs of the last row of seats in a state approaching ecstacy as Koussevitsky conducted with a fervor matching our own, Tchaïkovsky's *Pathétique,* or "the César Franck." At fifteen and sixteen we were by modern standards amazingly immature: I had cut off my braids that summer of 1926 and now had "a shingle," but Letty Field still had braids down her back, and our ethos did not include the masculine sex, whom we, on the whole, despised. Our emotional temperature was high, but we found release only in the imagination, and in the great flights of poetry and love that we poured out upon certain idols such as Katharine Warren, the actress, or Anne Thorp and Katharine Taylor, beneficent Muses for whom we burned the sacred fire.

Once a week or so we gathered at Letty's house, pulled down the shades, took out cigarettes, drank a muddy mixture made out of cocoa-mix plus a minimum of water, and then, smoking rather clumsily and coughing a good deal, read and dissected each other's poems with unmitigated severity. "I can't imagine anything worse than what you said about my poems, but I shall try to bear it," I find in a letter of the period.

I had begun to write poems seriously under Katharine Taylor in the ninth grade, for at that time she not only directed the school but managed to teach as well. It was natural enough from my point of view that I wanted to go on getting her criticism, and to keep her friendship after I left the school. From her point of view it was not exactly in the cards to have to be the Muse of a young poet, the teacher of a clumsy duckling trying to become a swan, and the adored friend of a former student all rolled into one. It never occurred to me that to ask for help, to demand attention, as I did, was to ask a great deal. But I know now that for her to find time to talk to me about life, love and poetry, as she did, was little less than miraculous. Possibly this was the beginning of my true education, education through fastening imaginatively onto a human exemplar and learning through love. What Katharine Taylor did, with extraordinary wisdom, during those years when I was emerging as a writer, was to temper the *exaltée*, discipline the heart, if you will, and through analyzing and criticizing my fumbling first poems, through the subject before us, help me to emerge from a sentimental vision (which naturally found expression in a sentimental style) to something harder, clearer and more honest. If Agnes Hocking brought me into the world of poetry, Katharine Taylor suggested that its essence was self-discipline and not self-indulgence.

In the midst of all this rich life, highly romantic and critical as we were, the High and Latin School appeared to us to be a kind of useless prison. The *Idylls of the King* seemed wholly unreal after Carl Sandburg's *Chicago;* I had devoured all the Waverley novels in one summer at Ogunquit when I was eleven, so *Ivanhoe* seemed childish. Life and education were separated, as we thought, forever. There was no relation between them, except that, though life might be "education" (and we had proof that it was), education no longer seemed to be life. It was just an albatross we carried round our necks.

What had happened, of course, was that we children of the twentieth century had been suddenly moved back into the nineteenth, to a school where nineteenth-century standards of learning were taking a final glow under a few excellent teachers. But we were indifferent to that slightly decadent glow in the blaze of our fresh convictions. The contrast was vivid between "prepare lesson three in your textbook" and the writing of a play in Latin, as we had done under Mrs. Reynolds at Shady Hill. Then we had relished the curious sounds coming from our barbarian mouths. Now Latin had become a "dead" subject. We had come from a school where we had been taught to examine ideas, to take nothing for granted, to ask a great many questions, to consider, in fact, that we embodied the dignity of the inquiring mind, the sacred destiny of man. It was clearly a part of this responsibility to fight every inch of the way if we did not believe in what was going on around us. The other night I was reminded again of this quality of the Shady Hiller when the daughter of a former schoolmate of mine laughed, and said, "Of course we were all trained hecklers." Our respect for the High and Latin was not increased by the fact that we did rather well from an academic point of view, and that we did not have to work hard to achieve this end. We had every advantage over our fellow students, and not the least of these that we regarded books as our natural friends rather than as our natural enemies. But we were saved, I hope, from becoming the insufferable snobs we might have been, by the skin of our teeth—by the violence of our passions.

Occasionally we were roused to fury, as when I came to English class one morning with the idea of doing a free theme on Ibsen, whose plays I had just discovered at the Boston Repertory and in Eva Le Gallienne's unforgettable production of *The Master Builder*. The subject for a free theme had to be passed on by the teacher, and when I revealed my intention, she flushed to the roots of her hair, as if I had uttered a blasphemy, and said, "You can't do that. Ibsen is immoral." It was a major crisis and around it my rebellion against the nineteenth-century view crystallized and remained frozen for many a year. No matter that this teacher happened to have a sense of style, and was in many ways more than adequate. I would be blind to her virtues from now on. I walked out of the room, went straight down the long corridors and down two flights of stairs and demand d to see the principal, gentle, wise Mr. Cleveland. There I stated my views with the courage born of rage, but whatever the private result (Mr. Cleveland was a very soothing presence), no public avowal of prejudice or ignorance on a teacher's part could be made, and I did not forgive. At that moment I ceased, except within the minimum outward necessary conformity, to be a member of the school. I became a revolutionary outsider, holding Ibsen to my breast as perhaps a later generation would hold James Joyce.

We had our heroes, too, among the students. One was Hermann Field, Byronic figure with his fair classic head, open shirt collars, and that fervor which has carried all the Fields into lives of nonconformist adventure, humanity, resilience. Hermann edited the school magazine, *The Cambridge Review*, a serious quarterly devoted to book reviews, poems, and short stories, and entirely humorless, I fear. He ran a series of poetry contests with book prizes as bait. Our allowances were at that time a dollar a week at most, and our appetite for books was insatiable, so the prizes were coveted. I remember my delight in a leather-bound copy of Millay's *A Few Figs from Thistles*, and the thrill of possessing Stanislavsky's *My Life in Art*.

It is strange to remember that world, to see Hermann as he was then against the Hermann Field who was released a few years ago after spending five years in a cellar in Prague as prisoner of the Communists—though, true to Field traditions, he emerged uncorrupted and bringing with him a magnificent novel, *Angry Harvest*, which has since appeared. Our world back there in 1926, 1927 and 1928 was radiant with hope. We pinned pictures of Woodrow Wilson up in our studies; "The Russian experiment," as it was called then, seemed to us rather like a gigantic Shady Hill where everyone would have a chance to become himself through serving a community in process of creation, and it was only a few years later that I bought a Hugo Russian Grammar and imagined that I would go over with a "shock troop" of friends to help unload goods which were piling up outside Moscow during one of the crises in "The Five Year Plan." We lived in an open world, and though we had not seen the future, we felt that it must work. Politics was a form of poetry; poetry was a revolutionary cause.

I have suggested that those of us who chose to go to the public school did so for democratic reasons; but if we were democrats, we were singularly inept, and actually what we did was to establish an island of "foreigners" within the school, and to make almost no contact with anyone outside it. There was one exception, a girl whom we watched from afar and admired. Her name was Elizabeth Tracy. She reaped harvests of A's; she was always beautifully dressed—we barbarians, who had considered any kind of elegance ridiculously effete, had to revise our views. Besides, Ibby Tracy was an artist. After a while we managed to walk home "her way." But she always remained a phoenix, more beautiful and finished than we could ever hope to be. And none of us was surprised when, at a very early age, she was painting murals in various public buildings under WPA.

As long as our education was still in the hands of teachers, it was just as well that we met our match more than once in those three years. I salute Mr. Delaney, Miss Sullivan, Miss Hogan, Miss Ford, the contingent of Irish brilliance who scared and cajoled us into preparing our lessons. Miss Sullivan did more; she found time to give me innumerable private conferences and to go over (with what patience!) my extracurricular poems, and she was gently humorous about effusions that deserved no better. But the greatest teacher we had was Mr. Derry in Latin. This round-faced, smiling, bald-headed man, solemn or twinkling behind his glasses, persuaded us for forty minutes at a time that we owed one subject, at least, our closest attention. By the time we came to him and Virgil after two years in the desert with Caesar and Cicero, we felt for Mr. Derry extreme respect. It is something to teach Virgil to a class of sixty students, who would not dream that it could be a pleasure (at that time Latin was required for the College Board examinations), who know also that if one is "called on" it is safe not to be prepared for several days to come, who many of them use "trots," though we, pristine in our innocence, never stooped to this evasion of responsibility. Yet it was an unforgettable day in my life when Mr. Derry spoke briefly to the point as we arrived at the famous lines which begin *"Lacrimae sunt"* —famous lines as fresh to us as the day on which they were minted. It was one of those moments when a world of feeling and understanding swims up into consciousness. The great mysterious thing has been said by someone for all time.

I look back on Mr. Derry with gratitude, yet I was not at the time convinced, even by his art, that four years of inch-by-inch progress through the classics is worth the candle. We had traveled through a long and arid desert, it seemed to me, to arrive for a moment at those saving Virgilian tears.

And in my final year I discovered Alfred North Whitehead's *The Aims of Education*. It cost more than two weeks' allowance, but it was worth it. For here was authority at last, a voice from the clouds, which crystallized all my amorphous ideas in a pungent, irresistible form. I filled my prose notebook (small, fat, and very leathery) with such items as: "It is not fair to the architect if you examine St. Peter's at Rome with a microscope and the Odyssey becomes insipid if you read it at the rate of five lines a day." Or, "When one considers in its length and in its breadth the importance of this question of education of a nation's young, the broken lives, the defeated hopes, the national failures which result from the frivolous inertia with which it is treated, it is difficult to restrain within oneself a savage rage."

It never occurred to me that the author of these galvanizing truths lived right there in Cambridge where I lived—as soon believe that Belmont Hill was Mount Olympus. The fact that my wildest dreams and most furious resentments had been sanctioned in a printed book was enough. It inspired me to write a polemical essay about the high school. But although I carried this bomb around, and even tried it on a few editors, it never did explode. We were, after all, about to graduate, and I was absorbed in fighting out with my parents the next, unorthodox step in my education, for I was by then determined to be an actress.

The graduation exercises, the end of my formal education as they turned out to be, took place in Sanders Theatre, sacred to Symphony concerts. I do not remember that day at all. What I do remember is the rehearsal, when Ibby Tracy, class orator, and I, class poet, stood in the vast empty auditorium and suffered under the efforts of Miss Hartigan—true love of the senior class and director of the school plays—to make us understand that audibility in a public speaker is a virtue. She met, I fear, a rocklike obstinacy, as Ibby and I recoiled from "rendering" our pieces in an appropriate manner. Ours not to reason why, ours but to stand and mutter for the sake of what we believed to be our personal and inviolable "truth." It was just as well that the poem could not be heard. It was not worthy of Mr. Whitehead; it proved that I had not emerged unscathed from the nineteenth century, for it referred to my two hundred fellow graduates as knights in armor, about to go into battle.

Those years at the High and Latin came back to me with delayed impact twenty-one years later when I found myself for a brief interval trying to teach Radcliffe and Harvard students the rudiments of good writing. The shock was to discover the enormous change in the world, as well as the change in my own perspective. Did I not find myself laying down the law as intolerantly as possible about "dangling dependent clauses"? No Miss Sullivan or Miss Butler could have been more severe. But on the other hand, I found myself at the same time the solitary inhabitant of an open world. My students, ineffably conservative, eyed with tolerant amusement a teacher who had remained a foolish old radical. It was I, it seemed, who had stayed, so much in spite of myself, in the nineteenth century.

*Eva Le Gallienne as Masha in Tchekov's* Three Sisters.

# The Civic Repertory Theatre

I was fifteen when my father, little foreseeing what effect his action would produce, took me to the old Hollis Theatre in Boston to see Eva Le Gallienne and her Civic Repertory Company in Martinez Sierra's *The Cradle Song*. It was my first experience of serious theatre when there is some intangible spirit at work which transcends individual performances, when a company and a play together make a gift to an audience which is a gift of the spirit, and the audience responds on the same level. *The Cradle Song* is a play about a nunnery, the joys and sorrows inside the walls; it is not a great play, but it has a radiant quality of humor and compassion and it was a perfect vehicle for the Le Gallienne company. Having seen it, I was not to be the same again. I haunted the Hollis while the company was there, saw Ibsen's *Master Builder* for the first time, and then again, and again; saw also *The Good Hope*, a Dutch tragedy of the sea. I sent flowers backstage and followed them after the play, terrified by a female dragon who (for the best reasons no doubt) roared at me and told me in no uncertain terms that I had no business taking Miss Le Gallienne's time.

But I was beyond good and evil, in the grip of a vision of life, of what, suddenly, I knew I wanted to be, and I was not to be stopped. I broke through into the little dressing room with its photographs of Eleanora Duse, its gray cairn called Tosca, its smell of grease paint and verbena, and its presiding presence, Miss Le Gallienne herself, who sat at the big mirror taking off her make-up and asked me kind absent-minded questions, until in desperation I blurted out that my dream was to play Hedda Gabler. No one could have looked more remote from the cold elegant Hedda than this awkward adolescent girl, hair cut like a boy's, her whole person suggesting exactly what she was, a professor's daughter. The incongruity of the wish and the person who expressed it made Miss Le Gallienne laugh, and turn on me an amused, appraising eye. The ice was broken, and after that she asked me to come back several times, and we were able to talk. Miss Le Gallienne was not encouraging: no serious artist encourages the young, for the risks in any art are so tremendous that one has to be very sure of extraordinary talent to say more than, "If you must, then do." She did make it clear that if I wanted to make the theatre my life, four years in college would be a waste of time. And, of course, this was exactly what I wanted to hear: "He whom a dream hath possessed knoweth no more of doubting."

But to my parents, during the two years of heart-searching that followed, my state did seem like a "possession," and we all suffered. For two years the problem I had become was argued, while letters went back and forth to New York, and I fought implacably to be allowed to join the Civic Repertory as one of the Apprentice

[ *148* ]

Group. Finally the matter was settled, after one terrible scene in which my father had shouted "Never!" and banged his fist on the table. It was settled with a little gesture, typical of him, when he and I were standing in the lobby at Symphony Hall at a concert: he offered me a Murad and murmured, "Be nonchalant." He then took out of his pocket a letter from Miss Le Gallienne making a definite suggestion that I come to New York the following year. It only dawned on me a few minutes later that he was both admitting me to the grown-up smoking world (up to then I had never smoked a cigarette in his presence) and agreeing to let me have my own way about my profession.

It was, as I look back on it now, a most generous and imaginative act for my parents to set me free to choose my own path, a path which seemed to them both —and rightly—hazardous in the extreme. It meant that my formal education would stop on my graduation from high school; it meant giving up Vassar where I had been entered, giving up college in a country where a college degree is mandatory in landing almost any job. I had to earn my living and they knew what a precarious living theatre provides, except to a very few. And for my mother, it meant letting her only child go out into the world very young indeed, probably not to come home for years, except for a few days at a time. But they had themselves taken great risks as young people; they appreciated Miss Le Gallienne's integrity and the values she represented; and, never laying the slightest weight upon me of the wrench it was to them, these extraordinary parents of mine let me go. My father agreed to give me a small allowance to live on during the years of apprenticeship, and on Saturday night, August 31, 1929, I was on my way to New York alone. I was seventeen.

I did not sleep a wink. I suppose that, now I had won, I faced that night the full responsibility of what I had undertaken, and the ordeal ahead. Did I really have the talent? How is one to be sure? I had spent the last two summers of high school during the holidays, acting at a semi-professional Little Theatre in Glouces-ter, run by Florence Cunningham, who had worked with Copeau in Paris, and Mrs. Evans, a remarkable director. I had played a few small parts and not done too badly. But I was well aware that the gap between this sort of experience and a professional company in New York was immense. And I was comforted finally as the dawn came by the device of William of Orange which my father had so often quoted about his own work: *"Je n'ai pas besoin d'espèrer pour entreprendre ni de réussir pour persévèrer!"*

As I look back on this experience from the very dif-ferent world in which I live, now that I know that the theatre was not to be my real life after all, I think I see what happened and why my imagination was seized so powerfully. I did not want to be in the theatre so much as to be in this particular theatre. For what I had felt streaming out from the stage at the Hollis was not the glamor of one personality (however powerful) so much as something even rarer—and exceedingly rare in the theatre—the tangible proof of what serving an art rather than using it for one's own ends can mean to those involved. This is what I had to know to the limit of my capacities, share in, become part of. My first great love was, in fact, the Civic Repertory Theatre, that kind of falling in love which frees the deep creative stream and forces one to grow. I believe that my instinct was true—even though theatre was not to be my medium of expression in the long run—for what I learned in the next six years was essential; even the ultimate failure was perhaps essential, and could not have been replaced by anything I might have learned in the academic grove.

The Civic was no grove. It was a shabby, musty old house, saved by a fine proscenium arch and a stage high enough to fly scenery for four or five productions at a time, a necessity for a repertory theatre. It stood opposite the Salvation Army on Fourteenth Street, with a warehouse next door, and the Sixth Avenue El grinding past it at the corner. The old theatre was a relic of the days when Fourteenth Street was "Uptown," the center of New York's fashionable life. It had opened its doors May 25, 1866, as the Théâtre Français with *Nos Alliés*, a play in three acts by Pol Mercier. Later on in that same year Adelaide Ristori played *Medea* there; it was used by French and Italian opera companies. The traditions of the old theatre were international from the first, though now it appeared like an island from the past in the middle of secondhand clothing stores. But for Miss Le Gallienne, when she took it over in 1926 to house The Civic Repertory, the site so far from Broadway was an asset. It meant that we could sell tickets at a top price of $1.65 and the second balcony at $.50, and so draw on the great audience of foreign-born all around us, who had known just such theatres in their native cities, as well as on the many American-born students and lovers of theatre who could not afford Broadway prices. "The Civic," as we affectionately called it, was theatre for the people in

[ *151* ]

two senses: it was within their means materially speaking, and it relied on their hunger for great works of art, on their wholehearted response to the very best. From the beginning Miss Le Gallienne's faith that "theatre is an instrument for giving, not a machinery for getting" was the key to its atmosphere, that atmosphere which pulled a Harvard professor's daughter out of her natural orbit like a magnet.

I experienced the beginning of that wonderful autumn of 1929 in darkness, the physical darkness of the "house" during rehearsals; there we apprentices sat for many days before the huge empty stage where only a work-light threw shadows on the brick wall at the back. We watched the company rehearse Tchekov's *Sea Gull* and Claude Anet's *Mademoiselle Bourrat*, which were to open the season. This was a period of passive learning; we felt like pygmies set free in a giant world. But we were critical pygmies because of our ignorance, the arrogance of the young and ambitious, who imagine, of course, that they are geniuses and would become giants overnight if only someone would notice their existence. We sent out for cups of coffee and discussed the actors by the hour. We had not yet suffered what they were suffering before our eyes. A play during its early rehearsals, especially a play as rich as *The Sea Gull*, demanding every inner resource of its actors, looks particularly rough and hopeless. Actors at this point are like moths, rather blind, easily frightened into paralysis, putting out soft trembling antennae which can be fatally bruised. A director who fails to understand this may lose the truth of the play at the very beginning, and never recapture it. Miss Le Gallienne's method was first to read the play

[ *152* ]

herself to the assembled company, a reading which made no attempt to "act it out" (this would have been to impose characterization in a dangerous way) but rather to set the tone of the whole and its proportions. This was followed by more company readings than are usual, until the inner life of the characters and their relations to each other were felt and understood in every nuance, and all the meanings quite clear. Only then did the company begin to move about the stage, and to find ways of "projecting" what had been inwardly realized. Miss Le Gallienne very rarely interrupted a scene or a speech, very rarely shouted directions from the house. I can see her, small and quiet, walking down the aisle in the dark, then jumping up to the stage to talk to an actor intimately, without raising her voice. I have seen her angry about a technical matter but never where an actor was involved, not even at a grisly dress rehearsal of *Hedda Gabler*—being put back into the repertory for a few performances—when Tesman simply did not know his lines. She was not angry then, or if she was, she did not show it. She simply set to work to teach him the lines, with inexhaustible patience—the actor was Paul Leyssac, and his Tesman, of course, was a memorable one.

Like hunting dogs straining at the leash, we who sat in the dark theatre and watched could scent something we did not yet fully understand, that slow pulling together of a company at work on a play, the way the whole emerges piece by piece, day by day, until all these pieces suddenly fit together and flow. Like hunting dogs we had our hours of boredom, but we also experienced the prick of excitement when we leaned forward after a long bumbling session and saw the miracle happen.

But we were not only passive watchers. We were attending regular classes in fencing under Santelli in the hours before the regular eleven-o'clock rehearsal began, and sometimes arrived early enough to watch the end of Miss Le Gallienne's lesson. She believed that fencing was the best exercise to develop an actor's stance and physical control, and she herself, lightning-quick, tense and adroit, was an excellent exemplar. It was amusing to watch her pitted against Santelli, with his Cyrano nose, who roared and teased her as unmercifully as he did us. They were not easy lessons.

We were also beginning to rehearse our own plays, rehearsals that had to take place after the company had gone home, late at night or very early in the morning, so we were often sleepy. We would, later on, be used as "supers." My first appearance before the footlights was somewhat inglorious, as I was completely muffled up and concealed from sight in the costume of a wolf in *Peter Pan*. Muffled is a mild word; I could see nothing, and had infinite trouble keeping the flashlight which worked the wolf's glowing eyes, lit up. I ran across the stage, totally blind, wondering whether I would reach the other side or fall off into the orchestra pit. But on the opening night I sweated it out in my wolf habit with a classic attack of stage fright. This initiation was still far off. Meanwhile I waited, and watched, and learned, and dreamed, as we all did. The school—and a marvelous school it was—was open without fees to the talented, chosen on the basis of a yearly audition (in the final years there were as many as eight hundred applicants for fifty places). You earned your way—you did not pay for it—earned it by playing in crowd scenes and small parts. In that early year we apprentices were about twenty in number, mostly from the boroughs of New York, though there was one from the Far West and one from Virginia. Our backgrounds varied from the poorest, materially speaking, to that of a girl who was sometimes driven to the battered stage door in her grandmother's Rolls. Arnold Moss, Burgess Meredith and Howard da Silva were members of the group that year. After the first weeks we were fully engaged in our own first production, Gorki's *The Lower Depths* with Egon Brecher from the permanent company as our director. Brecher had come into the American theatre some years before from Vienna, and had played Solness and John Gabriel Borkman with Miss Le Gallienne before the Civic was founded. He was a powerful and tyrannical director, and we were nervous beginners. I was to play Natasha; this part involves a piercing scream and floods of tears, neither of which I could produce. Rehearsing a scream presents difficulties. If I had done it in the tiny room where I lived at a working girl's club on MacDougal Street, the matron would have come rushing in. On the other hand, the stage was nearly always in use, and if not, there were sure to be people around, and I was frightfully shy. I finally found the solution in the old El. I used to stand on Sixth Avenue, just under it, and wait for its obliterating roar over my head: then for a few seconds I could scream in peace. I have no memory of the final production. I was still, as it were, swimming under water, so tied up in knots with incompetence and terror that even a performance hardly shocked me into full consciousness.

[ 155 ]

Our performances were given on the empty stage with a few necessary props, an occasional piece of scenery borrowed from one of the regular productions, and Henny Linck, the master electrician—and a genius—doing his best for us with lights. The costume department, two long rooms in the building next door to the theatre, yielded up costumes from its store. Members of the company kindly helped us with make-up, and then went out into the house to watch the performance.

When the curtain came down, we gathered on the stage, trembling, and Miss Le Gallienne, facing the anxious semicircle of apprentices around her, sat behind a little table and told us what was what. She was absolutely honest with us: the criticism was severe, inclusive and exceedingly helpful, though we were still too ignorant to put it to immediate use. Rarely indeed did anyone receive the accolade for which we all thirsted. More often we were acutely aware of the gap between what we had accomplished and what we had dreamed of doing, or perhaps had an intimation that we might one day be able to do at a single lucky rehearsal. Later on other members of the company would take us aside and give us their advice and encouragement. I remember Jo Hutchinson's warmth and kindness, and Leona Robert's shy, humorous and always-to-the-point criticisms. We knew that, however little we could show it, we were learning a great deal.

Meanwhile the company plays were moving toward the opening night of *The Sea Gull*, and the 1929–30 season. We had watched the growing pains, had learned the play by heart by this time, had been critical of or responsive to individual performances, but we had not seen the whole flower in an actual performance before an audience, the excitement in the lobby as the first-nighters gathered, the critics taking their aisle seats, and we ourselves standing at the back while Zarkevitch and his orchestra tuned up for the overture—for no theatre worthy of the name lacked an orchestra, in Miss Le Gallienne's view. Now the theatre where we had sat so many hours in the dark was alive and alight with attentive human faces. What wonderful audiences they were! The orchestra might not always be sold out, but the second balcony almost always was, and these students and secretaries, these shopkeepers and clerks bringing their memories of an Art Theatre in Kiev or Vienna, were our real joy. Years later when the theatre had been pulled down and become a parking lot (had it all been a dream?) I found myself on the corner of Fourteenth Street one day, and stopped at a tobacconist to buy cigarettes. His face lit up when he saw me, and we spent a half hour together remembering performances he had seen, "the good old days" when you could see Ibsen, Tchekov, Shakespeare, Giraudoux played by such actors as Nazimova, Ben Ami, Joseph Schildkraut, Eva Le Gallienne, Josephine Hutchinson, Egon Brecher—for fifty cents.

On the opening night of *The Sea Gull* we knew for the first time what the Civic meant to the community, and we were bursting with pride. But as the lights dimmed and the gold of the high proscenium arch gleamed softly, as the "foots" came up and the asbestos curtain rolled its ugly self away, as Zarkevitch led his orchestra in a final gallop, we forgot the audience, we forgot everything but the play itself. Had we ever seen

[ 157 ]

it before? No, never. There was Masha—not Miss Le Gallienne, Masha—dressed in black, slightly stooped, saying, "I'm in mourning for my life. I am unhappy." We forgot Robert Ross's struggles with the difficult opening speech of Tryeplyev and only felt the tension in him as he paced up and down and suddenly broke out, "My mother is a psychological curiosity." We were swept into our first experience of that human, humorous, compassionate world of Tchekov so beautifully balanced, like life itself, between tears and laughter. When the curtain fell that night, after the curtain calls and bravos, and after the audience had gone, a few of us still sat there with Jo Hutchinson's voice ringing in our ears: "I do know, I understand, Kostya, that in our business—whatever it is, acting or writing—the chief thing isn't fame, isn't glory, not what I dreamed of, but the capacity for taking pains." We held all the reverberations of the last hours to our heart's ear as if the play were a shell in which we heard for the first time the murmur of the ocean.

In that year we saw the curtain rise on eleven different plays from the repertory: sixty-three times on *The Sea Gull;* thirty-three times on Tolstoy's *The Living Corpse;* twenty-six times on Claude Anet's *Mademoiselle Bourrat;* sixteen times on Molière's *The Would-Be Gentleman;* thirty-eight times on Barrie's *Peter Pan;* twenty-five times on the Quinteros' *The Women Have Their Way;* three times on Ibsen's *Hedda Gabler,* five times on *The Master Builder;* and—this was pure luxury—one each on *John Gabriel Borkman* and that extraordinary play of silences, Jean Jacques Bernard's *L'Invitation au Voyage.* The season ended with a triumphant production of *Romeo and Juliet.* We were beginning to under-

[ 158 ]

stand what repertory means, this library from which one treasure after another is drawn, as well as the enlivening experience it is for actors never to play the same part two nights in succession. A typical week that year might run *The Sea Gull* and *The Women Have Their Way* on alternate nights, with matinees of *Peter Pan* and a single Wednesday-night performance of *Hedda Gabler*. This was for us a real education in the theatre. There is nowhere in America now where it could be obtained in that full measure.

It is not only that the theatre as a whole has had to fight for its existence against the implacable demands of the craft unions (though now the off-Broadway companies are finding ways to put on productions for less than the minimum sixty thousand a Broadway production costs). But the world outside suffered, of course, a violent change in the year of 1929–30. The Civic Repertory like any symphony orchestra or any of the great European repertories such as the Comédie Française, depended upon subsidies, and in this country such subsidies come traditionally from private enterprise. It had not been easy to maintain a theatre for the people when money was flowing freely in the boom times before the crash. After 1930, as the margin almost disappeared, it was to become harder and harder. Miss Le Gallienne was not only playing demanding roles, rehearsing, directing, and supervising the productions, managing the whole complex organization with its hundred or more artists and craftsmen on the payroll, but she had also to raise the money with which to carry on. She was still in her early thirties and she had astonishing vitality, but it is no wonder that she seemed to grow slighter and her eyes more enormous as the years of this strain went on.

I have seen few actors who live as intense an inner life upon the stage as does Eva Le Gallienne. Others who are said to have done so, like Eleanora Duse, rarely played a full week at a time, the psychic expenditure is so great. Here again repertory is invaluable as it rests the player by means of its variety, and makes it possible for him to come with a fresh response to each performance, neither to grow stale, nor to become depleted. Eva Le Gallienne could hold an audience breathlessly still for as long as a minute (very long on the stage) by the sheer intensity of her inner life, projected. I am thinking of a moment in *The Master Builder* when Hilda faces Solness's jealousy of a younger architect, and Eva Le Gallienne as Hilda sustained a very long pause before uttering the words, "That was a very ugly thing to do"; or the moment in *The Cherry Orchard* when Varya kneels by the little trunk, waiting for a proposal of marriage which is not spoken. At such moments the actor's concentration must be of a very high order; he communicates a whole sequence of feeling and thought, a lifetime, without a single word or a single gesture. He must, in fact, be able to communicate his soul, and he must have a soul to communicate. The trouble is that, when one has seen acting of this intensity and depth, one has acquired a hunger for a kind of nourishment which the theatre today almost never provides.

I was part of the Civic Repertory for three years, first as an apprentice, the following year as a member of The First Studio, a small group of apprentices chosen to go on for a second year (we produced Jean Jacques Bernard's *Martine* on our own in the Repertory); and finally after a year in Paris when the Civic was temporarily closed, as member of the company and director of the Apprentices. If I had to choose one image of all those that crowd in when the name "Civic Repertory" is spoken, I think it would be the annual Christmas performance of *Peter Pan* that we gave as a present to an audience of orphans. I graduated from a wolf to an Indian, then to the invisible star Tinker Bell (a mirror in my hand that flashed a tiny figure of light over the stage), and finally to a "speaking part," Lisa, the little maid who helps Peter Pan in the tree house. Then I had the great thrill not only of speech at last, but of flight, for Lisa, you remember, strides her broomstick, cries "Home, James, home!" and flies off through the tree-tops.

We were used to enthusiastic audiences, but this houseful of children, many of whom had never been inside a real theatre before, was something else again. When Captain Hook dropped poison into Tinker Bell's glass, many of them rushed down the aisles, shouting, "Look out, Tinker Bell!" During the fight with Captain Hook, they even tried to climb onto the stage to help Peter win. Their roars of laughter met one like a solid wall. The old theatre rocked with emotion, and when Eva Le Gallienne as Peter suddenly flew out into the midst of them, almost to the balcony edge on the final curtain call, thousands of hands reached out as they tried to catch her, and a huge sigh swept after her back to the stage.

Someday there will have to be another such theatre, rich in great plays of all nations, open to the mass of the public, providing a school where young actors can serve

[ *161* ]

their apprenticeship, and where even a young writer may acquire something more valuable than a college education, the sense of what any art demands of its servants, the long discipline in the craft, the devotion, the selflessness, the power to endure.

*"Lugné-Poë...this creature on a huge scale, so avid for life, so generous in his welcome to it..."*

## That Winter in Paris

I look back on that winter in Paris as one might
look back on a period of illness or even insanity, or
perhaps simply as one looks back on oneself at nineteen.
It was the winter of 1931–32—I had spent the preceding
two at the Civic Repertory Theatre as Apprentice and
member of the First Studio, but the theatre was temporarily closed. My parents were off to the American University at Beirut, where my father would continue his
Arabic studies, and I was left in Paris, by my own choice,
to fend for myself, to study theatre, and (it was supposed) to take advantage of the monuments of civilization that lay all around me. There they were—the Sorbonne where I might have studied, the museums, the
libraries, the cemeteries. I stood before them like a cat
with one paw raised, unwilling to step into cold water.
I did nothing wise or sensible. I simply lived in Paris.
I wandered about, ardent and hungry, picking up whatever was accidentally brought to my attention, tasting
it and then wandering on, casual and solitary, always it
seemed on pavements with a film of damp over them,
my feet half frozen, wearing my only respectable gar-

ment, a purple corduroy suit, with a copy of Baudelaire —bought for five francs at a stall—in my purse. I read this, as perhaps it should be read, on benches here and there, in cafés when I was suddenly too tired to walk another step. Whatever I learned, I learned, as Henry James put it, from "the rich ripe fruit of perambulation." It was Paris by osmosis.

Of course, I had to live somewhere, and the somewhere turned out to be Montrouge, a workmen's quarter, just beyond the Porte d'Orléans, for a friend sublet me his apartment there, on the Place Jules Ferry, where there were a few blocks of modern apartment buildings. My place, in one of these, was, like that whole winter, curiously empty and curiously crowded. It was chiefly a studio, empty except for a large glass bottle made into a lamp, a mattress on the floor beside it, a phonograph, and some records—my friend was a dancer. The living quarters, on the other hand, were on a small balcony above this chill vacuum, and they were extremely crowded, containing as they did a bed, a desk, bookshelves, chairs and a fireplace. A tiny kitchen and bathroom opened off on one side of this balcony, and on the other side it gaped draftily onto the unheated studio. This strange apartment was on the ground floor, and I lived there, acutely aware of every footstep on the pavement outside, with no companionship except for a mouse who came out at night and ate crumbs off the carpet by the bed.

The chief trouble with living in this quarter was simply that the Métro shut down at midnight, and if I went to the theatre or was out with friends, there was nothing for it but to take taxis; my budget hardly allowed for such extravagance. But living on the Place Jules Ferry had one great advantage. There was market once a week, just outside my door. On that day I woke to the sound of wooden trestles being put up and the harsh cheerful cries of the vendors, and I woke up in a village. As in all such markets, you could buy anything from rubber boots or a sweater to cheese, vegetables, meat, and fish. When I emerged with my basket, it was into a friendly, busy, talkative village scene, and I was welcomed: *"Hé, mon p'tit, v'la le meilleur p'tit tricot vous verrez de vot' vie—ça tient, tu sais, ça ne s'use pas,"* the ever-hopeful sweater woman yelled from across the square. My best friend was the egg man, who handed his customers a little basket and said in the softest voice, *"Choisissez, Mademoiselle—un p'tit oeuf à la coq, rien de meilleur, n'est-ce pas?"* I was fond also of the cheese woman with whom I had long talks about which was superior, La Vache Qui Rit or La Vache Sérieuse at twenty centimes more. It was 1931, and the franc was at roughly thirty-five to the dollar. I bought eggs, cheese, sardines, tomatoes, and always a bunch of flowers— bunches of cheap marigolds or daisies, and once in a great while, early in the month, roses.

What astonishes me now—surrounded as I am, as we all are, by a network of responsibilities—is the utter freedom of that year, the freedom not to do, as well as the freedom to do. I spent hours listening to records, writing poems and letters, keeping a rather helter-skelter journal, or just lying on the mattress in the studio, feeling happy, feeling unhappy, romantic, directionless, ready to veer with any breeze. I was, of course, making vague attempts to learn about theatre. I got permission, for instance, to visit the rehearsals of the Compagnie des Quinze, then in its first burst of glory and preparing for a season that would include Obey's famous *Noé*, and to visit rehearsals of the Pitoëffs whom all Paris adored, though I myself, insensitive perhaps, could not share the enthusiasm for Ludmilla. I saw a great many plays, for Jouvet and Valentine Tessier were playing at the Champs Elysées and Dullin at his "Atelier" (in a wonderful production of *Volpone*). I went back three times to see the haunting, hieratic Marguérite Jamois in Gantillon's production of *Maya*, the prostitute who becomes the incarnation of each man's secret dream of woman. But the thing was, of course, that I was burning to act myself, not just watch others perform, watching them as I did with the sour, absolute, critical eye of inexperience. "Where is the theatre?" I cried disconsolately, brushing all these riches aside.

I wanted to break in myself. Secure in the armor of ignorance, I cooked up a wild scheme and dashed off a letter to Lugné-Poë. I suppose that Lugné-Poë at that time might have been compared to a combination of Belasco, the entire Theatre Guild board of directors and Alfred Lunt rolled into one: Entrepreneur, director, actor, it was he who had first introduced Paris to Ibsen, who had founded and directed the Théâtre de l'Oeuvre, and who even then kept consistently in the *avant-garde*, discovering a new playwright or a new star each season. His name was still magic in the Paris theatre. It was magic to me for a rather curious reason. For I had, three or four years earlier, fallen in love with the tiny Vuillard portrait of Lugné as a young man, the face bending over a desk, the cap of black hair, and the whole stance (only the shoulders, head, and hands being visible) suggesting intensity of a very high voltage. I knew also that he had played Solness in Ibsen's *Master Builder* many times since he had first produced it in the 1890's. My letter was a barefaced request that he revive it and allow me to play Hilda opposite him.

Of course, I never really expected any result from this piece of effrontery. It was the kind of letter you write when you are nineteen and suspect your grandiose schemes of being exactly what they are, screens against despair. It was like the poems I was writing at the time, a way of persuading myself that I existed. So when the public phone in the hall rang a few days later, I went quite calmly to answer it. A deep masculine voice asked for me by name, then said, "*Mademoiselle, vous êtes folle,*" and invited the mad demoiselle to come and have a talk at his office in the Rue Turgot: it was, of course, Lugné-Poë.

The Rue Turgot was in a section of Paris I had not yet explored, and to get there I had to change two or three times in the Métro, so it seemed quite an expedition when I set out the next morning. If I were to choose one single thing that would restore Paris to the senses, it would be that strangely sweet, unhealthy smell of the Métro, so very unlike the dank cold or the stuffy heat of subways in New York. The smell of the Métro is more than a smell: it is an aura, an emanation as powerful and unlike anything else as is the breath of a cow, and to a lover of Paris it is intoxicating. I was properly intoxicated when I finally emerged into that warm sunny November day, into a quarter I did not know, on my way to meet the man of Vuillard's portrait. The Rue

Turgot is a dingy little street with the usual cold façades that open into courtyards, the usual little shops, shoe-makers, or mustard vendors, and when I came to the number I had been given, I looked twice because nothing here had the faintest resemblance to a theatrical producer's offices.

A little boy in a black apron and sabots was playing with a bucket and shovel in the courtyard. I peered up a dingy staircase and then turned back to ask where I could find Lugné-Poë. "Monsieur Lugné is not here yet," the little boy answered in a high soprano. It was warm, and I was tired. I sat down on the stoop beside him, and for some reason I have forgotten put the pail on my head for his amusement. I was sitting there in that ludicrous position when the child nudged me and said, "*Voilà!*" Lugné-Poë wore a large black hat and seemed enormous and formidable. He did not look amused as he glanced at us. He was followed by a male secretary carrying two brief cases, and they disappeared up the dingy staircase while I received the full impact of my own foolishness and arrogance and would have liked to melt away. But the whole thing had been a dare to myself and I had to take it. I followed them up the narrow dirty stairway to the second floor. The door was open. It was always open, for the office was so small and so packed with books, papers, magazines, manuscripts, files that there was barely room for Lugné-Poë in his big black leather armchair and for his roll-topped desk stacked with piles of dusty telegrams. (They were all from Eleanora Duse, relics of Lugné's management of her South American tour, as I learned later.)

I sat down without courage and endured a long

piercing glance from those black eyes. Then we both laughed, and I found myself talking with him, quite frankly, quite simply, as if he were an old friend, about my ambitions, my loneliness, my longing to play Hilda. It was an examination, but at a certain point in the examination I knew that I had, for some quite unknown and fantastic reason, passed. During the course of it, he told me that I had the face of a writer, but not, he would think, that of an actress; he had found out that I wrote poems and demanded that I send him some within a few days; he had told me that if I was determined to keep on in the theatre against his hunch, he would see if he could get me a walk-on somewhere, and meanwhile that we would keep in touch, that he would not forget me. While we talked, the secretary popped in and out from the back room, getting more and more exasperated, because he was trying to reach Ruth Draper for Lugné, and had been given a wrong number. "Try 92-91," Lugné would say, and then, when that did not work, "Well, try 19-29," and while they worked at this hit-or-miss system, I could look at the big man who sat so relaxed in his armchair and who did not resemble the Vuillard portrait at all. The young man Vuillard caught thinking would never open a huge mouth and laugh that devouring laugh; nor did the man in the painting look like an elephant, as Lugné-Poë, with his great sensitive nose, his immense forehead and small sardonic eyes, certainly did. He was altogether smaller and tighter, the man in the portrait, than this creature on a huge scale, so avid for life, so generous in his welcome to it in whatever form, even the arrogance of the young.

When finally I was out on the street, I did not know

whether I felt more deflated, reassured, befriended, or challenged, but surely some of the loneliness had been lifted away. He did not forget me, for he had, as I was to learn through the years, a genius for "keeping in touch" with those he had chosen, or who had chosen him, all over the world. And what a company it was, international by the accident of birth, but closely allied in that they were all actors, playwrights, poets, artists, all in need of his laconic "Bravo!" telegraphed from Oran to New York, or his, "Look here, my child, despair is not in our genre. Besides, you cannot disappoint me. We have work to do, you and I."

He did not forget me in that first winter of our still tentative friendship. I was summoned to attend a dress rehearsal with him, or just for a talk in the little office, or for his suddenly shy, always perspicacious comment on a poem. I would not admit that I was to be a writer and not an actress—that would take six more years— but since I would not admit it, he was willing to wait and believe in what life itself would do. And meanwhile he was educating me, thrusting a play in manuscript into my hands, insisting that I read and perhaps translate Lenormand, always divining the moment when the little donkey I was needed a carrot.

And I was learning in sudden flashes. I had never heard the word "surrealism" when I went to the first showing of Cocteau's film, *Le Sang d'un Poète*, but the shock of beauty and strangeness produced in me a riot of conflicting emotions that were acted out before my eyes by that first audience in no uncertain terms. All during the film people shouted insults at each other, got into actual fist fights, subsided, whispered furiously, walked out, came back, by the intermission were mortal enemies, and by the end were magnetized by their quarrels into knots of gesticulating furies in the lobby. I had not realized what passions art can arouse until that evening, and it was exhilarating.

By the middle of the winter, I had established certain relationships and had a few real friends. One was Mary Chilton, who lived in a pension on the Rue Notre Dame des Champs, where I had stayed briefly before getting settled in Montrouge. Mary Chilton was studying at the Sorbonne. She was seventeen, shy, intensely serious, and studied late into the night. I used to pass by the pension on my way home from a theatre or from those interminable discussions at the Café du Dôme a few blocks away, and if Mary's light was still on, I would throw pebbles at her window, and she would come down and unbolt the door and let me in. Then, at midnight and into the small hours of the morning, we sat and talked by her open fire. I admired her tremendously. She was, I sensed, a true intellectual. She had the distinction of extreme sensibility with a hard, disciplined core. We enjoyed each other because we were so different. She was following a definite program of reading, for instance, while I picked up books here and there in the stalls, and made sudden discoveries—Virginia Woolf's *The Waves* (just out), Péguy, the Shaw-Terry letters, Rimbaud. When I think of that winter in Paris, it is Mary who first floats before my eyes, the stillness of the night, her soft voice, her dreadful pallor—for she was actually seriously ill, though we did not know it—above all, her clear blue eyes. Our two solitudes never quite merged, perhaps, but accepted each other gratefully. She represented for me a kind of innocence and depth that I, in my new-found sophistication, so unsophisticated actually, felt I had already and forever lost.

For while she studied, I danced, or went to the theatre or to the Médrano Circus with other friends. The Fratellinis were playing that winter. Who will ever forget them? One was the classic clown straight out of the *commedia dell' arte*, sad and beautiful, with his stark white face under the white conical cap, red tragic mouth, surprised doleful eyes; he wore a brilliant spangled suit, yellow or crimson, with a round white collar, white shoes and socks. Their act began with his entrance on a pro-longed trumpet fanfare. He stood before us, absolutely still, and slowly lifted his arms straight out in a wide stylized gesture of—was it acknowledgement of the roar of applause or a kind of ovation to the joy of what was to follow, this grave, this noble gesture? It made a tremor run through the audience, and on the current of that tremor the two other brothers, the grotesque ones, ran in, one in the guise of a horse, perhaps, his huge flopping shoes showing beneath, the other in a worn top hat, play-ing a tiny violin. They had the indefinable magic quality I have only seen once again, in Harpo Marx. They came from another world, dancing and playing and inventing their preposterous jokes, and whatever they did was magic.

My other great friend was also American, a young stage designer whom I had known at the Civic. She lived in a beautiful attic room in the Hotel Foyot. It had a slanting roof and its mansard window opened onto the tower of the Palace in the Luxembourg Gardens and its comforting clock face. When we had been out too late

[ *172* ]

for me to catch the last Métro, I sometimes stayed the
night with Irene. We ordered scrambled eggs and coffee
sent up from the restaurant downstairs, where we could
never afford to eat a real meal. Always short of money,
we used quite often to have supper at a café near the
Odéon, eggs and a salad. Then we would make a brief
appearance at the *Cochon de Lait* next door, and order
( to the undisguised horror of the waiter ) nothing except
coffee and their wonderful *mousse au chocolat*. What
barbarians we must have seemed, and in fact were! Our
idea of a really good drink was that perfect period piece,
the Alexander cocktail.

We were enamored of another period piece, the in-
destructible Stroeva, who sat on a high stool, in a tuxedo
with glittering studs, and sang sentimental French songs
in a heavy Russian accent, accompanying herself on a
guitar. We were a little late, for she had enchanted
Scott Fitzgerald's generation and it was they who
hummed those tangos—"Tu Sais," for instance. During
that winter Stroeva sometimes appeared at music halls
like Bobino's, which we could afford, but more often at
an intimate night club on the Right Bank near the
Opera, which was outside our sphere in every way. It
must have been embarrassing to her to see us arrive
night after night during the period of our infatuation,
in the same suits, one purple, one bright green (everyone else in evening dress, of course), take the same table,
pay the minimum charge, and sit in an intoxicated silence, broken only by our frantic applause at the end of
each number. But we were Americans, and Americans
were scarce that winter. We were treated with admirable
courtesy.

There were less embalmed evenings when we danced to an accordion in the joints on the Rue de la Montagne, where the customers were not Americans, but were regular Parisian toughs, leading from the hip and bending their *mômes* far backward in the tangos we all loved. There I went with a Dutchman, bespectacled and earnest, who watched me and the French with the cool eye of an anthropologist at large, and whom I remember with gratitude because he gave me as a parting gift his heavily underlined (in red ink!) copy of Gide's *Nourritures Terrestres*. ("All the tiredness in your head, Nathanaël, comes from the diversity of your riches. You don't even know which among them all to choose, and you don't understand that the only riches are life itself. Nathanaël, you must burn all the books.")

There were hours of immense excitement when, after browsing under the arcade of the Odéon bookstall, I ran off with my prize "to burn it in myself" in the Luxembourg Gardens—a worn copy of Colette, Péguy, Stendhal, or Joubert, the leather binding falling apart; or the poems of an unknown who turned out to be well known and whose name was Valéry. There I sat in the shade of chestnut trees, late into the autumn while the leaves whirled up in eddies around me, cutting the pages, stopping to look out at the high plume of the fountain and the children sailing their boats in the round pond at its feet. I cannot ever go back without remembering that here I first discovered Stendhal, here Péguy. Everything I saw around me flowed in and out of the printed page, the wide sandy paths where mothers and children and old men take their places and become part of the formal pattern as if they were kings and the mothers and children of kings; the serrated palaces of leaves in the air over those odd truncated busts of the Queens of France, and over it all the ever-changing mountains of cloud, the Alpine scene which melts and reforms all day over Paris.

Like so many other Americans and English who have made up a Paris of their own, this was my Paris, but it hardly was a Frenchman's, and I knew almost no French people at that time. Like nearly all Americans that year, I was poor, for it was 1932. Our personal letters were full of the news of jobs lost, of businesses closing down, of men selling apples in the streets. By a curious stroke of fate, I did not lose a job that year but was offered one.

For Eva Le Gallienne was convalescing in Paris after the nearly fatal explosion of an oil furnace in her house in the country; she had been burned within an inch of her life, and was emerging from the agonizing comeback. Her presence in Paris was a particular joy—it was she who had taken me to see the Fratellinis; she invited Irene and me to a Christmas celebration in her apartment on the Rue Gît-le-Coeur, and in the atmosphere of holiday, of time, I was able to talk with her about the Apprentice Group of which I had been a part, and about the future. Suddenly one night as we sat at a café table, she suggested that I take over the direction of the Apprentices and offered me thirty-five dollars a week (a fortune to me at that time). It was what I had hoped, but the hope had seemed as wild as my letter to Lugné-Poë and, when I saw it realized, I could do nothing but burst into tears. She also gave me for Christmas a beautiful pen, made of amber with a silver band on it and my initials, and I have often wondered if this was not because she suspected, as did Lugné-Poë, that my real life would not in the end be in the theatre. At any rate she had showed some of the poems I had been writing to her father, Richard Le Gallienne, and from him I had the first professional response, the first intimation that this secret part of my life might have some reality for others. No praise, no prize, no recognition later in life can ever mean what his letter did, for as Ruskin puts it, "It is only the young who can receive much reward from men's praise . . . you might have brought the proud bright scarlet to their faces, if you had but cried once to them 'Well done,' as they dashed up to the first goal of their early ambition." Richard Le Gallienne did just that for me, and I carried his letter around in my purse until it was worn out.

Meanwhile I could go to Lugné-Poë and tell him, in triumph, that it was, after all, to be the theatre. But the job was still a half year away, and at the end of each month Irene and I were always flat broke, always in debt, and cooking up schemes for existing until next month's checks arrived from our families at home. One of these schemes has stayed in my mind as, in some way, the essence of that irresponsible winter. In a moment of desperation, we decided to pawn the various objects of value that Irene's friends and admirers had given her over the years. In Paris, where life is so highly individualized, it came as a shock to discover that pawning was official business, conducted by the government in an institution that resembles both a prison and a bank. The walls were bare; there was nothing to relieve apprehension except a row of *guichets* that looked like ticket windows in a small New England railway station. All around the walls sat silent pale-faced people, who might have been prisoners about to go on trial. They waited with tickets in their hands. We were subdued at once by the atmosphere and took a last hunted look at the gold compact, the cigarette case, the silver mesh bag that we hoped would make us solvent again. They were duly passed in to a man at a ticket window, and we sat down, clutching our tickets and feeling more and more like criminals. Presumably, while we waited, some bureaucrat noted down the objects in a great ledger, pausing with his pen in air, as they all do, and for some reason fashioning each letter in air just above where it would go down in ink on the paper. Presumably, several corridors away, someone else in a Prince Albert coat put a magnifying glass in his eye, and assessed the value of each object. At any rate, whatever was going on behind the wall took an unconscionable time. But at last our number was called and we were filled with a wave of hope.

What was the clerk telling us? And in such a severe tone of voice, too, as if we had been trying to cheat the government. "These are worth nothing, Madame."

"But the silver mesh?" Irene managed to protest.

"Imitation."

"The gold compact?"

"Silver gilt."

We gathered up the poor familiar objects which had lost all their glitter in an instant and slunk out of the door. Then Irene laughed, a bit ruefully no doubt, but she did manage to laugh.

We came out into the early spring air, the damp

[ *177* ]

streets, the flower woman at the corner selling narcissus and mimosa from the south of France. We came out into the trembling rainbow atmosphere, and it all swept over us as if we were seeing it for the first time. John and Arthur, or whatever their names were, those faithless swains who had given Irene silver gilt for gold, were forgotten, and we consoled ourselves by buying a small bag of *marrons glacés* with our last few francs. After all, we were in Paris, and it was a lovely day.

The other image which remains with me as the essence of that time is quite a different one. It was a day of national mourning, the day of Briand's funeral. Whatever his blunders, his sentimentality, his old-fashioned sense of the destiny of France as a civilizing power, his belief that war could be "outlawed" by a pact that rested on the moral force of world opinion had been a positive unshakable strength. His generosity vis-à-vis Germany had suggested the possibility of a new era in Europe. When he died, even such ignorant, self-absorbed young people as we were felt a kind of premonition, the shadow over the sun.

All along the Champs Elysées the lamps were lit, and each shrouded in black gauze. All along the Champs Elysées the people had gathered—people who had made expeditions from the suburbs with their children, people who just happened to be passing by, people moved by the desire to see a parade, foreigners, French. We all waited restlessly as traffic was detoured and the wide avenue became suddenly empty and still, pivoted on the two triumphal arches, from the Etoile to the Louvre. For such a crowd, we were curiously silent. We shuffled, we waited, a father scolded a little boy who wanted to

be held up to see—"*Mais, voyons, il n'y a rien à voir.*"
Then, far off, we heard the drums, then the slow march
as the bands began to play. The Garde Républicaine's
helmets caught the light and flashed in the distance, then
came past, the guards holding their horses to a walk,
the bits jangling. Battalions of soldiers followed, still in
horizon blue (it was the last time we were to see it),
and finally the casket itself, draped in the tricolor, moving slowly enough so that the dignitaries at its side could
keep in step, sashed in red, wearing their rows of medals,
the President and Cabinet, the foreign ambassadors, the
generals. Each time the casket itself reached a group on
the sidewalks, a kind of sigh went over. We were saying
good-by to a world, and strangely enough, for that brief
moment, we knew it.

The Paris of that winter seemed empty to us, and I
felt for years afterward that I had wasted it. Now it
seems very full. It is already the past, the irrevocable
past. Mary Chilton died that spring, quite suddenly;
Lugné-Poë, just before the fall of France; the last of
the Fratellinis is gone. Good-by, my Paris. But someone,
nineteen now, is sitting in the Luxembourg Gardens,
creating a world within that world, and tasting the "rich,
ripe fruit of perambulation" in the ancient ever-renewed
and renewing city.

## Impossible Campaigns

The Civic Repertory closed its doors for good in the spring of 1933, and the Apprentice Group, which I had been directing, was left dangling in thin air. We were young, earnest, convinced that we wanted the kind of theatre in which we had grown up. There was remarkable talent among us, including two apprentice directors, Eleanor Flexner and Kappo Phelan. Why not try to keep together for a few years? Our chances on Broadway would be slim indeed; might we not make our way in an altogether more fruitful, learning climate if we could work as a group? As H.T.P. wrote so discerningly a year later, "Along their way they seek discipline, adventure and association. They would gradually acquire the resources, certainty and pliability which discipline brings; enjoy the adventure of stimulating parts in taxing plays; cultivate the association that makes a theatre-company a sensitive, reciprocating instrument." Was there any choice? Lifted on our wave of enthusiasm and belief, we thought not. We named ourselves The Apprentice Theatre and spent hours in Child's, just around the corner from the Civic, laying plans. They were modest

*"Within a year my first book of poems was published...
from that time on I never looked back."*
DRAWING BY POLLY THAYER FOR *Encounter in April, 1936*

enough—to find a place where we could live and work together for a summer of rehearsals, and to collect somehow the few hundred dollars we would need for food and lodging.

These came to us, as so many miraculous interventions did in the beginning, through the contagion of the dream. Angels appeared out of nowhere. An old school friend from Shady Hill, Katrine Greene, handed over to us a legacy of five hundred dollars she had unexpectedly received, and we were lifted on those generous wings right out of New York to Dublin, New Hampshire, to a rickety old house other generous friends lent us for a minimal rent, for that first summer. There was even a barn nearby where we could rehearse on a stage, and in addition to providing the means with which to do it, Katrine offered to come and run the house for us. We arrived, a motley group in a series of ancient cars, unloading books, records, broken-down armchairs, sheets, typewriters, chess games—we were far too delighted and excited to notice that our descent upon rarefied, Proper Bostonian Dublin was not much less alarming than would have been the entire Joad family from *Tobacco Road*. I heard later that the house in which we lived that summer so happily, and which we immediately christened Tchekov House, was torn down shortly afterward though the reason was never mentioned. Fumigation was not apparently considered sufficient!

We had, however, powerful support from Katrine's parents. Rosalind and Henry Copley Greene cared passionately about the kind of theatre we hoped to create; they understood our problems, as well as being able to laugh at both our foibles and the Dubliners'. They had

[ *181* ]

the imagination to see that a rather stout young man who chose to walk around Dublin Pond in nothing but bathing trunks and carrying a huge stick should not be regarded as an orangoutang on the loose, but a normal human being out for exercise. By some extraordinary fact they even persuaded the Club, which provided the only swimming facilities on the pond, to take us in as a group. There were periodic alarms raised in the village about our presence, but the Greenes quelled them and I was only aware many years later of what they endured as a buffer state.

For us it was a halcyon beginning. The old house shook with music, laughter, tempestuous arguments, philosophical discussions and plain hard work. I find again the enthusiasm, the sense of discovery in my letters to my parents: "Last night we worked in the theatre by lantern light on some experiments. It is perfectly beautiful at night. The experimental work is really the test of the group; so far we have had two periods (one every other day). Two of us invent a set of problems for the rest to act out. It is an extremely intense hour. It always ends in discussion, but the extraordinary thing is the real creativeness of the group, and their sufficient love of the *end* to take very severe criticism from each other and *use* it (which is even harder). Their power for sustained concentration amazes me." These were problems to develop group playing and might, for instance, have included a scene on a street corner where two gangs of teen-agers meet, almost clash, and swagger off instead in opposite directions. There has been an enormous lot of this sort of thing going on lately off Broadway, but twenty years ago we were the avant-garde; the off-Broadway theatre hardly existed.

All day we were hard at work rehearsing our first two productions, H. R. Lenormand's *A Secret Life*, which I had brought back with me from Paris, and Schönherr's classic *Children's Tragedy*, which Eleanor Flexner had translated. "But, outside work," as I wrote at the time, "there are thousands of things going on. Burrage is great on organizing baseball; Hank Green spent yesterday in a pair of shorts squatting in front of a typewriter composing 'the log.' In one corner Scourby and Bill Phillips are playing chess; in another, a dancing class is doing exercises; and on the stone wall at the back, Margaret English is roaring at the Heavens, 'Whisper, ye winds, that Hunca Munca's mine!' " —rehearsing her part in Kappo Phelan's production of *Tom Thumb*, which she had designed with her usual flair with all the actors on stilts but for Margaret, Tom Thumb himself. Unfortunately this production had to be laid aside when our plans for the winter jelled.

I had been looking around for a stage on which we could play in New York, could get some audience reaction and criticism, without embarking yet on professional production. The more I thought about it, the clearer it seemed to me that we had two assets, which together, might provide the solution: thanks to Eleanor's knowledge of German and Theodora Pleadwell's and my knowledge of French, we could make our own translations of plays that had not yet been seen in New York; and we had become accustomed as apprentices at the Civic to "rehearsal performances." Far from needing the expense of production, we might capitalize on our capacity to do without it. And the very absence of scenery and costumes would emphasize that we did consider ourselves "apprentices." I wrote to Alvin Johnson, director of the New School for Social Research in New York, asking whether he would be interested in offering ten modern European plays as a course at the school. It would give us a chance for a rich variety of experience at almost no cost; it would give the students the opportunity to see these new plays alive instead of merely reading them. It was a wonderful day in early June when we got final word confirming Mr. Johnson's approval of the plan, and offering us $1,000 for the season.

Now the whole pace of the summer accelerated. I had my first taste of the terrors of responsibility, for somehow enough money must be raised to pay each of us the minimum twenty dollars a week on which we could just manage to live, and that meant four thousand over what Alvin Johnson could offer. It was the middle of the depression. I remember well one of the many talks I had with Abraham Flexner, Eleanor's father, and his rueful smile as he told me that a few years earlier he could have raised the necessary sum with a few telephone calls, "but now . . ." I wrote letters to everyone any of us knew who might be persuaded to invest in a wild dream, and to many people we did not know. Friends came forward unasked; and little by little, in small trickles, in occasional fountains (notably a miraculous thousand from Joseph Verner Reed), we got together enough to make the venture possible. There was never exactly peace of mind, but in those years of constant anxiety, I learned to trust to fate and not to despair as long as we could buy baked beans and coffee for one more week ahead.

Meanwhile, in Dublin still, we were beaverishly happy, designing and building a set of large black screens and plain black boxes (reminiscent of Henry Copley Greene's gray boxes at Shady Hill) that could be shifted around to make skeleton sets. I did have moments of wondering how we would manage to get ten plays on in that one winter, but there was very little time for worrying: we were swept along by the work itself.

At the end of the summer we invited our friends and neighbors to come and see performances in the barn of the two first plays. Both *The Secret Life* and *The Children's Tragedy* are somber difficult plays, and in our cocoon of self-absorption and dedication, it never occurred to us that their impact on a summer audience of Dubliners might be devastating. I do not know, but I feel pretty sure that the evening was one of almost unmitigated suffering and shock for our guests. But we were blissfully unaware, and the Greenes, at least, felt that the summer's work had justified our hopes.

We had before us a different, more professional ordeal—a run-through of the first three plays for Eva Le Gallienne and Alvin Johnson on the Civic Repertory stage in New York. Miss Le Gallienne had given us her support, qualified by her knowledge that we were unlicked cubs, indeed; and though we called ourselves "The Apprentice Theatre," were in fact not apprenticed to any master in our craft. She had generously offered to give us her criticism, and did everything in her power to help. We did have the sense to appreciate the grace we were allowed in her willingness to sit through three

[ 185 ]

long plays and then to tell us all that we needed to learn. It was a tremendous fillip on that memorable afternoon to hear that she felt we had all grown over the summer, and then to be given the sort of precise, clear criticism each actor and director could devour and use. And our cup was full when I heard from Alvin Johnson the next day, "I knew your company was good, but I did not know it was as good as it actually is. We shall be very proud to have you with us."

After our first performance at the New School, I could write home happily, "It was really an excellent audience, about two hundred people, sensitive and quiet, and the actors outdid themselves. I felt proud in a new way at the real distinction of each separate personality that came on the stage. Harold Freedman came *again*. He thought the play had grown since he last saw it, and altogether kept talking about the extraordinary imaginative impact of the performance. S. N. Behrman was also enthusiastic."

The plays followed each other at roughly two-week intervals, and I am quite astonished when I look over the series at what we managed to do. Let the list speak for itself:

| Nov. | 6th | *The Secret Life*—H. R. Leonormand |
| Nov. | 20th | *The Children's Tragedy*—Karl Schönherr |
| | | *Still Life*—Ferenc Molnar |
| Dec. | 4th | *Naked*—Pirandello |
| Dec. | 18th | *Dr. Knock*—Jules Romains |
| Jan. | 15th | *The Call of Life*—Arthur Schnitzler |
| Jan. | 29th | *The Sowers*—Jean Giono |
| Feb. | 12th | *Martine*—Jean Jacques Bernard |
| Feb. | 26th | *Fear*—Alexander Afinogenov |

March 12th   *Gentleman Wanted*—Walter Hasenclever
March 26th   *The Armored Train*—Vsevolod Ivanov

It was a great year. Critics and producers came down to Twelfth Street to see us; we were "noticed"; and, above all, we were learning enormously in the doing. What might have seemed a liability—the fact that we played without scenery, make-up, or costumes—turned unexpectedly into a triumph: people were more impressed than we deserved, perhaps, that such an illusion could be created with such restricted means.

But these attentions from Broadway producers and critics, though gratifying, carried with them the seeds of danger. Individual actors began to be singled out, to get nibbles or actual offers of professional jobs, and the soul-searching decisions had to be made, whether to go or stay. At the end of the season two of our best actors, Norman Lloyd and Alexander Scourby, decided that they could not afford another year with us. At the time this seemed to me rank disloyalty, not on a personal basis, but to our idea, for our whole plan had been predicated on a five-year period of working together, to be followed eventually, we hoped, by a formal debut on Broadway, bringing with us new American plays. But I see now that these early defections were inevitable. I could not even pay a living wage. More important than money, a young actor does not have infinite time; he must get there fast or perhaps not at all; in a profession where luck plays so grim a part, it is madness not to take your luck when it is there.

There were to be losses all along the way, but we also discovered new young actors, and one professional "star," Eliot Cabot—who had learned what Broadway looks like from the inside—offered us his services for the second summer, to direct and produce Shaw's *You Never Can Tell*. I was delighted to welcome him, for I was eager to find a director for myself as an actress, and I was very conscious of the danger of the company becoming a one-man show. It had been from the beginning my responsibility, but there was a danger that I might cease to be useful because I was forced to do too many different things, not only acting and directing, but raising money, finding plays, actors, places to work and live—and above all carrying on the constant search for a base outside New York where we might serve our apprenticeship and build up an audience.

For our second season we were offered a charming little theatre in the Wadsworth Athenaeum in Hartford. There I hoped to begin to produce new American playwrights, and to that end I must have read two hundred plays without finding one that was suitable. I suppose as many bad novels are written as bad plays, but it is hard to believe. At any rate, Hartford was our first venture into real production and we learned the hard way what costs become when scenery, lighting and costumes are involved. I look back on that winter as a long struggle to raise money, illuminated here and there by moments of joy: I think our first production, a French adaptation of Plautus's *Menaechmi*, was the most finished and elegant performance we ever gave. But the company was naturally restive; there was really not enough to do. They were cut off from New York, and we did not succeed in luring sufficient support in Hartford to imagine that we could root ourselves there.

At this point wisdom might have led me to reread a letter Eva Le Gallienne had written me when I first decided to launch out on the Apprentice Theatre. She said, "I have thought a great deal about all you said when you were here that day—and you know how eager I am to support and encourage any individual *initiative* in the theatre. At the same time in my thoughts for your own future, I can't help wishing that you could have a few years of gruelling work in somebody's company, not mine, so that your foundation was a bit more solid. I do feel too from my own experience, as well as from observation, that to have won one's spurs in an individual way in the regular (and often horrible) mill of the commercial theatre, is an enormously helpful thing, before starting to fight the windmills of Idealism. It implies a *free choice* from *richness*; you will understand what I mean."

I was not wise. I was stubborn, convinced that persistence and belief would win out, and, perhaps unluckily for me, I was still able to convince others. When we disbanded in Hartford, our financial situation was desperate, although our last performances, in which I played Hilda in *The Master Builder*, were sold out.

We would need a minimum five thousand dollars to embark on a third season, a place to rehearse for the summer, plays, a business manager, and above all a theatre in which to make this last attempt. I spent the spring desperately trying to find backers, and very nearly gave up. But at the eleventh hour one last miracle happened. I was invited by the Herbert Lymans of Boston to spend a weekend at their house in Northeast Harbor and to speak to an invited audience, among whom they hoped a substantial sum might be raised. It was the last throw of the dice; with what fear and trembling I took the train! The Lymans had invited twenty or thirty people to dinner, and I spoke afterwards. In the front row an elderly man with very intent blue eyes sat and made notes. I did not know who he was. And after what appeared to be a swan song, the charming guests came to shake hands, one by one, and to say how regretful they were that they really could not help. When everyone had gone, and I was trying to compose my mind to accept the end, Richard Cabot, the man who had taken so many notes, came up and said very quietly, "I would like to help. Come and see me tomorrow morning and we'll have a talk." I was battered, exhausted, and in very low spirits when I climbed the rocky path to his house in the woods back of the Lymans'. But Richard Cabot was a man who could give people wings. In half an hour, fixing upon me his intent gaze, and asking me just what was necessary to launch us, he promised five thousand dollars to be on call as we would need it.

Once more the little company gathered, this time in a rented house at High View, New York. The owners fed us in the big farmhouse, and converted their barn into a rehearsal theatre. It was a beautiful place "with a view almost as good as the plain below Assisi." Alexander Scourby and Norman Lloyd agreed to come back for that season; I had found at last a man who, I hoped, would turn out to be a real co-director—Waldemar Kappel, an Austrian who had worked with Max Reinhardt and who would direct me in our first production, a play he had chosen called *Gallery Gods* by the Austrian playwright, Richard Duschinsky. The second production was to be Jules Romains' *Dr. Knock*, directed by me, and with an excellent starring part for Norman Lloyd. We had trouble with the third production, but finally got permission from Maxwell Anderson to revive his play about Sacco-Vanzetti, *Gods of the Lightning*, and Jo Losey came up to direct it. I had a new young business manager, and altogether hopes ran high, in spite of some casting difficulties and a good deal of tension within the company as a result. We now called ourselves The Associated Actors Theatre, Incorporated.

We were to open in Boston for three weeks on November eleventh and to go on from there to a little theatre in Brooklyn. No one could foresee, when the dates were set for Boston, that in the same week, Katharine Cornell, Eva Le Gallienne and the Russian Ballet would all be playing there! This was enough to spell disaster. But on St. Crispin's Day I got this letter from Richard Cabot and with it as our *devise* we gathered on the shabby stage at the Peabody Playhouse for our first night:

"Dear May,

My name is Henry Fifth and at Harfleur:

'I see you stand like greyhounds in the slips, straining upon the start. The game is afoot!

*Follow your spirit* and upon this charge cry:

'God for Harry, England, and St. George!'

My business is to set you free for that charge. Let me see you run. That is all I want and it is much for

your affectionate backer

Richard C. Cabot"

Alas, our "running" was brief and disastrous. We played each play for a week to audiences which sometimes were no more than ten, and at the end of the three weeks Richard Cabot's five thousand dollars had vanished. I do not believe that these productions were as bad as this disaster might imply. But I do believe that we had come to an end of one phase, the apprentice phase, and were not ready for the next phase, professional production. Further, in the long run, all companies such as this must discover new playwrights if they are to justify their existence (on a much larger scale, *The Quinze* had introduced André Obey, and The Group Theatre, Clifford Odets). Neither *Gallery Gods* (a play about actors) nor Maxwell Anderson's early *Gods of the Lightning* were quite good enough as plays; and as a company we were not quite good enough to put them over in spite of their weaknesses. We had reached the end, and I knew it.

It might have been a clean break with some of the exhilaration that the acceptance of failure brings with it, not unlike the exhilaration of accomplishment; one clears the decks. But unfortunately there was bitterness and recrimination to be faced and dealt with: my co-director at one time thought he would bring the company together and go on without me. The break was confused and poisonous, and I suppose that is why I have until now blocked out those three years completely.

Now, as I assess it all from a distance and from the security of moderate achievement in another world, I have been rather surprised to discover how much we did accomplish. The first year at least was, by the standards we set up, a success. In the end we failed for the reasons Le Gallienne had suggested in her letter: we had bitten off more than we could chew; our belief was out of proportion with our capacity, at the time.

Let me speak for a moment of what all this meant to me as a human being apart from my role as a theatre director and as an actress. What did I learn from it? What did I take with me from it into my life as a writer?

First of all, an intangible: it is not a bad thing to have to face total failure at twenty-four. It toughens the spirit and makes one aware that, though all may seem lost—as, indeed, it did seem—human beings have unquenchable resources within them. I was lucky, of course, in that during all those years in the theatre I had been writing poems. The first ones had appeared in *Poetry Magazine* when I was still an apprentice at the Civic, and I had never ceased to feel the compulsion to express myself in words of my own, as well as on the stage. Within a year my first book of poems had been accepted and published by Houghton Mifflin, and from that time on I never looked back. I was exchanging what Richard Wilbur has called "not impossible campaigns" (those of a poet and novelist) for what had proved in my case to be plainly "impossible" campaigns in the theatre. During the days in which I have been reliving this piece of the past, I have been haunted by the final stanza of Wilbur's poem *The Good Servant*, and perhaps it is a fitting close to this chapter:

> Above the ceded plains
> Visored volition stands
> And sees my lands in chains
> And ponders the commands

Of what were not impossible campaigns
If I would take my life into my hands.

I had learned that I had certain powers of leadership
and of communication that would from now on involve
continuous choices. But these choices would be far easier
than if I had had no experience of power. That temptation, at least, would not seduce me, the temptation that
might have led me into full-time teaching, for instance, as
once it had into directing and producing. For teaching,
curiously enough, is one of the human concerns in which
power is nearly absolute—just as directing in the theatre
is—for someone who knows is watching and criticizing,
kindly or unkindly, the fumbles of someone who does
not know. Perhaps it is this early experience which has
made me extremely wary abut any position of power,
and led me to take the eccentric position that creative
writers should not become reviewers, because so much
power is immediately involved. I am convinced that a
creative artist must remain as free as possible from any
commitments except that arduous commitment to his
own work. He may be a critic as Virginia Woolf was, or
as T. S. Eliot is, as one of the means toward clarifying his
own ideas about his craft. When he becomes a reviewer,
he is down in the marketplace where he does not belong.
I deliberately chose poverty and freedom. But poverty
would seem ease, would seem luxury, compared to the
nightmare of continuous money-raising I had experienced. I had a growing sense of inward strength that
had nothing whatever to do with any signs or tokens of
outward power. When failure came again (as it must to
any serious artist) I was not afraid of it. On the positive

side I had a tool in the ability to speak in public and to "project" to an audience, which would prove to be useful in communicating the inner life of poetry to college audiences in the years to come. I have no feeling of waste about those six years in the theatre.

At the end of them, I was no longer the shy, gauche, romantic young girl who had fallen in love with a theatre, and had crashed her way backstage. I was beginning to be myself, and to know who and what that self was. And in this sense, my education was at an end. In almost every other sense, it was just beginning.

## Two English Springs

It was as if, in that spring of 1936, I were emerging from six years of a strange and illuminating illness, which had its own value but which had isolated me almost completely from the normal life of a young woman. Perhaps it is not a bad thing to be preserved in amber, as it were, till the ripe age of twenty-four. For when I was suddenly free of the burden of responsibility, the sensation of lightness was intoxicating. I had closed the door on the theatre, but another door was opening into the intensities of a private life, of time, of solitude, of poetry. No awkward debutante who suddenly finds herself the belle of the ball could have been less prepared for life than I, more taken by surprise, more open to any delightful and fortuitous event. And in this mood I landed in England, alone, free, and totally "disponible" as Gide would say.

It began in a storm of green rain, a rich infusion of spring after the gray limbo of a March Atlantic crossing. I landed at Plymouth to spend a few days with friends of my parents before assaying London on my own. There at the station in Par, Cornwall, Charlie Singer who had been for me only a name, the "great English historian of science," was suddenly transformed before my eyes from this abstract essence to a beneficent Teddy bear, with curly white hair and a shrewd, kindly smile. As we bumped along through sheets of rain, he briefed me on Cornwall (where the Phoenicians had come on expeditions for tin) and announced in the same breath that Julian Huxley (on a no-less-vital errand) was to be a fellow guest for the weekend. Huxley was then Secretary of the Zoological Society and had come down to see about the possibility of growing eucalyptus *en masse* for Koala bears, who cannot live without immense quantities of fresh leaves every day. Charlie told me this as if growing acres of eucalyptus for a few small bears was quite the usual thing in Cornwall, and I was prepared to believe it, for everything under the sluices of rain, had an air of phantasmagoria about it.

We arrived at Kilmarth in the dark, a flashlight spotting daffodils and primroses in the long wet grass, and—was it possible?—a snow of camellias falling through the air. I looked up and saw that we were not only treading a tapestry of spring flowers, but stood under camellia trees as large as elms. The driving rain, the smell of earth, the wild wind, this wet green world stormed by petals, made together a violence of spring such as I had never imagined, and shall never forget. It affected me like some great burst of sacred music, the opening of a Haydn Mass. I stumbled into the house in a daze.

The weekend was a series of shocks. In England, I soon learned, windows are kept wide open even in the middle of a hurricane, and one dresses for dinner, especially in the depths of the country. The Singers are exuberantly kind hosts, but I was wrapped in strangeness like a cloak. After breakfast on that first morning, sitting opposite the Huxley eyebrow, quizzical, slightly Mephistophelean, I had just extricated myself enough from my own acute shyness to laugh at a joke, and taken out a cigarette, when Charlie reached over and slapped my wrist. "You can't do that in England," he said. I felt the blush rise in waves from my toes to my throat, to my forehead, and tried to imagine what taboo I had broken. Did no woman smoke in England? Or was it merely so dreadful just after breakfast? Or what? I vanished into my stranger's cloak and did not speak or move till we rose from the table.

It was still raining, though the wind had fallen. We were marshaled for a walk, encased in mackintoshes, armed with rubbers and canes, and driven to the border of an abandoned estate, which had been allowed to run wild for twenty or more years. There we got out and began to penetrate into what looked like jungle, and in an hour moved from Himalayan brooks where rhododendron towered, to forests of bamboo that might have been Malaya. We gazed up through a roof of flowering laurel to immense jungle-growth of English beeches, found ourselves in an avenue of camellias walking on carpets of white snow, and came out into glades of classic English spring, where bluebells grew so thick they made blue pools. We went up and down and round-about while Julian Huxley, a long-legged stork, darted here and there whooping with delight, or—silent as an Indian and as concentrated—tracked a bird, naming off and calling back to us the individual songs he could distinguish from

[ *198* ]

what sounded to me like an indistinguishable chorus. When we stopped for a moment in a misty grove of bamboo, someone remarked that it would not be too surprising to meet an elephant, and Charlie told us how, on another occasion when another visitor had made the same remark, an elephant did appear, trundling along waving his trunk—an escapee from a passing circus. Since everything seemed wholly improbable to me at that moment, an elephant would have been only another sign that the magic wand was at work, the wand that had set me down here in the first place, in the middle of my first English spring.

At last we climbed out of the jungle part of the estate to the ghostly house itself, a Victorian pile, surrounded by lakes of grass, by grazing sheep, by ancient English oaks, and covered with flowering japonica. We climbed up onto the terrace and peered through the windows, and there intact was a complete Victorian world, untouched for fifty years, sending us back our own reflected faces, as if we ourselves were ghosts being summoned from a distant past. I did have the sensation all through that weekend that I was dreaming: What was real? What was unreal? But I woke up sharply when Julian Huxley, as he left for his train, wrote down his telephone number on a card and invited me cordially to come and see him and his wife at the zoo. What an adventure!

Then I lost myself in London. I found a furnished room near Baker Street—brown walls, brown bedcovers, a sooty window opening onto sooty "backs"—where I stayed in bed writing all morning to save shillings on the gas meter, and in the afternoon walked and walked, in ignorance, dismay, curiosity through the streets and parks, wondering sometimes if I existed. This suspension of one's own reality, this being entirely alone in a strange city (at times I wondered if I had lost the power of speech) is an enriching state for a writer. Then the written word—those black squiggles that one moves back and forward like counters on a page—takes on an intensity of its own. Nothing gets exteriorized or dissipated; all is concentrated within. And up to a point, such isolation can be fruitful. But before I got too lost in it, I had a piece of luck, and fell by accident into the perfect London lodgings. I was able to sublet the large comfortable bachelor room of a member of a co-operative household at 23 Taviton Street, in Bloomsbury. This was an establishment jointly owned by a group of professional men and women, who had separate rooms, led separate lives, but could, when they wished, share the ministrations of a joint cook for the modest sum of ninepence a dinner. Breakfast was a silent meal, each member ensconced behind his newspaper, but occasional glances over the *Times* led to occasional invitations to tea or dinner in a restaurant. The chief members when I was a resident were a professor of physiology at the University of London; a historian and critic of architecture whose room adjoined mine and who played Bach on his harpsichord by the hour to my delighted edification; a woman Doctor of Medicine; a theatre designer—and who else? Here memory fades. I am alone, happy and alone, in my vast room with its tiers of empty bookshelves, its few beautiful old pieces of furniture, its table by a large window, where I realized, "how precious it is to be surrounded by *sympathetic* furniture" after the dismal gloom of Baker Street. I could afford bunches of anemones and wall flowers and tulips now and then; I had a private musician next door to play for me.

I am aware that the words "alone" and "solitude" and even "loneliness" keep appearing on these pages. They have the sound of happiness about them, and in fact, being alone was one of the major reasons why I was happy, for in the theatre years I had almost never enjoyed that luxury, time to think, time to be, time to pursue an image, an idea down through the layers until it yielded up its essence. I remember that room as all light and peace, cool impersonal light, the peace of the temporarily suspended person I was.

Of course there was the whole of London outside, for the tasting, for the exploring. The Huxleys lay dormant, a card like a talisman in my purse. Possibly I sensed that the times in one's life when one is as uncommitted as I was are rare, and precious. I had no obligations, even to friendship. I was writing poems about trees ("beech and laburnum, saffron fountains, the candled chestnut, the ballerina elms, the hawthorn curving pink umbrellas over lovers"), about the London parks, a festival in themselves; there was Russell Square just down the street where I once saw Virginia Woolf leaning on Leonard's arm, under an umbrella. When it rained, there were the museums: my first discovery of Piero della Francesca, and the delighted recognition of that small mysterious landscape ascribed to Patinir; my first discovery of Oriental art, for it was the year of the great show of the Eumorphopoulos collection and I went back three or four times. The list means little, but the images it evokes are still intense for me, because one sees paintings best when one is lonely. I spent hours browsing in the open barrows of secondhand books along Charing Cross Road, bought Arthur Waley's translations of the Chinese poets, the charming Constable pocket editions of Katharine Mansfield, the Sidney Webbs' hopeful tome on the structure of society in the new Russia, and above all Gerard Manley Hopkins's poems and letters, that I had not known.

Although I have often regretted my ignorance, there are advantages in having escaped a formal college education. One has the excitement of the explorer, who, although a million people before him may have stood on the same peak, experiences it in the full force of his innocence, discovers it for himself. When I ran into a writer like Hopkins, I did not rush through him to prepare for an examination in a survey course on English literature; I recognized him as a crucial contact to be explored as carefully and slowly as a new friendship. I had time to read everything he had written, to build him into my bones and blood. So it had been much earlier with Emily Dickinson, with Virginia Woolf; so it was to be with W. B. Yeats.

I came back from these expeditions into London to borrow my Bach-playing neighbor's teapot and cups, to make us strong cups of tea and exchange the day's news. My relationship with John Summerson—for that is who it was—was intense, but its intensity was expressed impersonally when I was writing in my room and he was playing music in his, the fortuitous exchange of two solitudes. We hardly talked.

I had, of course, amassed a small packet of letters of introduction, each of which seemed like an adventure in embryo, like a packet of seeds. Which to chose? Which to send? Each meant a journey by bus or tube to a different part of London, the perils of somber blocks of flats called "Gardens" or "Mansions." I soon learned that a Mansion address means the exact opposite of its name, and a Garden anything but a green place. One afternoon I set out to make the acquaintance of A. H. Fox-Strangways, music critic on the *Times*. The open sesame in this instance was a letter from my father, with whom he had shared a desk in the War Office in 1914 when they were both censors. They had worked side by side for weeks, never speaking, until the English ice was broken and a formal introduction through a mutual acquaintance could take place; after that they became firm friends. I remembered this tale and wondered what sort of camelopard I would find. Shaggy, perhaps, with a formidable beard? He lived in dreary "Gardens" I noted. I was not prepared for the exquisite creature who opened the door, for those transparent blue eyes, delicate porcelain skin, and the smile hiding itself behind a white mustache. The rooms I entered were dark, full of green baize coverings, books, an air of discreet poverty, and something elegant, nostalgic like a perfume from some earlier time, which I did not recognize as the classic emanation from a "younger son." His natural courtesy broke down before my barbarian accent; it was disconcerting to have one's simplest and shyest remark greeted with guffaws of laughter as if at an immense, perhaps even mildly off-color joke. It was clear that he regarded me, my rose-polished nails, and all my ways as one regards the representative of a primitive tribe: I was the camelopard. It was my first experience of English insularity *au pur*, and

I felt bruised. It was also the first disconcerting evidence that I belonged nowhere, a "half-breed," as I used to announce when I was a child, since my father was Belgian, my mother, English, and we lived in the United States. For many years I was to have this feeling of exile wherever I went, to be pulled back to Europe as "home" and then to feel a stranger there, after all.

Little by little, as I poured out for us innumerable cups of black bitter tea, and he discovered that I wrote poetry, and told me that he edited a journal called *Music and Letters*, and would be glad to see some samples, the frost in the air gave way to a mild winter sunshine. And finally he read aloud, as if I were Alice in Wonderland and must be entertained, from a tale which pretended to be a translation from the Sanskrit, and which made his mustache tremble with a more humane laughter than I and my American "accent" could evoke. We parted friends, and later on he did publish a poem of mine, "On Mozart and Keats," and so was responsible for my formal debut in England as a poet.

This was a fair sample of various encounters the letters of introduction provided. Another was my first vision of Kew Gardens in May, with Harold Stabler. Who can forget his first sight of Kew?: the close-clipped emerald grass where ducks sit motionless as porcelain, the ponds strewn about as precisely as if in a child's drawing, the long vistas through immense trees to the Chinese Pagoda, and above all the way the people, all sorts of people, all sizes and shapes, take on the air of choruses in an opera, moving as if propelled to music through these formal spaces. It was my first experience of the peculiar rapture formal gardens induce—and I remember hurrying home to try to get it down in a poem.

Finally I summoned the courage to take out one more seed from my packet, Julian Huxley's card, and made my way to the zoo in Regent's Park for tea. The Huxleys were living in an airy bower over the Administration Building. One went up, past offices and files, in a small elevator, to emerge suddenly into a pale green drawing room of the greatest elegance. It opened, in turn, onto a long glassed-in balcony and a lovely view over the great trees and lawns of the park. Inside were to be discovered all sorts of wonders; a gray parrot in a cage, sometimes two budgerigars allowed to fly about freely, and once when T. S. Eliot came to tea, a lion cub whose immense paws made the human beings present seem fragile indeed. Best of all, there was Gulliver, a bush baby, lightning clothed in soft mouse-fur with immense agitated eyes, who could leap from the top of the curtains to a shoulder with no apparent effort in a speed of motion like flight. After dinner he was sometimes invited in for dessert to sip chocolate mousse from a glass-stemmed dish, but one never knew when he would take to the air, or descend from a height to perch on a shoulder like an angel.

It is hard to pin down that first meeting, because I found in Juliette and Julian Huxley a grace, a charm, a way of making a stranger feel at home that melts that first occasion into many others, and into years of friendship. What I do remember was my delight in observing them together, for they would take almost any odd scrap of information or opinion and toss it agilely to each other like a ping-pong ball, an airy, teasing game, punctuated by bursts of laughter, until Juliette after a particularly daring sally, put her hands up to her face and said, "I have shocked myself." As an only child I had fallen in love often with families; and now as an unmarried young woman I was falling in love with a marriage. There is a Spanish greeting, I am told, that says, "Tell me your life and miracles," and one of the miracles of my life was surely this meeting.

When I came back the following June, the Huxleys lent me their apartment at the zoo in Whipsnade, that green hill thirty miles from London where animals rove in paddocks instead of cages, wallabies run about the woods freely, and with any luck one may see one, standing in a lake of bluebells, with a baby peeping out of her pouch. Parakeets fly wild overhead, and zebras thunder down a long green field; it does not seem startling to see a tiger fast asleep under a hawthorn tree. All week I lived alone in the comfortable apartment over the Zoo restaurant, and on weekends the Huxleys came up with their two boys, so I had solitude and society in perfect proportions. What a piece of imagination it was on their part to lend me this haven, as I embarked on my first novel! I worked hard all morning and then could rove about. The restaurant gave me a special rate as a regular customer, and happens to be a very good restaurant, indeed, not at all what one might imagine at a zoo; it was also beautiful, for it had long French windows opening to the Flamingo pond where wandering deer came to peer in.

The days were peaceful, the nights, faintly alarming. I would sit up in bed, wide awake, startled by the scream of a peacock (so like a soul in distress), or the ghostly hoot of an owl. Sometimes the wolves started howling. They lived in a dark wood of straight trees, the ground barren beneath their ceaselessly padding feet, and at night they looked like wicked ghosts. But in the early morning Whipsnade was pure delight; the dew still on the grass, no one but keepers about, it rose out of the dark like a vision of the Peaceable Kingdom. When I felt stale, I amused myself by taking chalk crayons and a sketchbook out and blunderingly trying to draw—especially one soft taffy-colored bear who loved to sit in the fork of a tree, her nose lifted to scent the air, and one paw lolling over a branch; she looked rather like a Maillol nude, but clothed in fur.

It was a wonderful month: concentrated solitude for work and dear companionship at the end of the week. And then the final fabulous fact of living *in* a zoo! There is one scene that remains in my mind as the meridian of this time. It was the Coronation year, and the British were busily entertaining various dignitaries and potentates from the Commonwealth, among whom was the tribal prince of a Nigerian principality. His name was, I believe, the Alake of Abeocuta, but as I never saw it in print, I cannot vouch for this. At any rate this tall smiling black man, dressed in ceremonial regalia, and followed everywhere by an attendant carrying a gold umbrella to shade him from rain and sun, captured the imagination. He wore a long gold cape, beaded boots, a round brilliantly colored beaded hat surmounted by a bird; he carried a scepter with a dove on the end, which he waved affably at the crowds who followed him wherever he went; and he radiated joy, dignity, and a pleasure in his own importance which has grown rare among crowned heads. He was followed closely by a cameraman who recorded on film for the later delectation of his subjects, every event in which he took part. On this occasion he was being escorted through the zoo by the secretary, Julian Huxley, and various dignitaries in top hats, notably Lord Lugard. Quite unaware of these eminences, I was working away in my room when Julian burst in, and said, "Come along!" and there I found myself among the top hats and golden umbrellas, in my old slacks and shirt. We were taken around in a bus, and I was given a V.I.P. view of the zoo with all the animals on parade. As we approached, the lions were thrown hunks of meat; the Alake himself reached up a long arm to feed the giraffe, and, best of all, the rhinoceros, usually so sedentary, was persuaded to gallop down his paddock. I have never been in Africa, but I understood then that one has no conception of a rhinoceros until one has witnessed that armed fortress in motion. The speed, the thunder of it was tremendous, and also (since we were safe) very funny.

After all this excitement had subsided and the princes and lords had been whisked away in their limousines, Julian took me to see Castor and Pollux, two cheetahs who looked exactly like the leopards one sees in Persian miniatures. We were allowed into the cage and, rather gingerly, I began to stroke Castor's round Teddy-bear ears. A roar began in his throat and I leapt away, terrified, until I saw Julian's smile and heard the keeper chuckle; the formidable roar had been simply a formidable purr of pleasure. As we sauntered back to lunch through the wallaby wood, Julian said, "Well, you have met the Alake of Abeocuta and made a cheetah purr all in one day!" Such are the joys of being a friend of the Julian Huxleys.

It was through them that I came to know S. S. Koteliansky, "Kot" as he was known to his friends, and Kot was to be one of the seminal people in my life. In that spring of 1937, he was not eager to meet new faces, but fortunately, since he was a reader for the Cresset Press, the manuscript of my first novel passed through his hands; he told the Huxleys that I had some glimmerings of talent, and they invited us to tea together. For me it was a momentous event: in the midst of all the excitements of those English springs, when I was just discovering myself as a young woman, and just opening my wings as a beginning writer, Kot appeared like warm fresh bread after almost too much champagne. He made great demands on his friends, but they were always demands in depth, demands that one be authentic. In his presence, emotions, ideas, fell into place; self-intoxication became self-searching. There was to be no nonsense, only "the truth"; and therefore a visit to him was something of an ordeal.

It was also a ceremony, planned by postcard or letter well in advance, and eagerly awaited on both sides. It was wise to be early rather than late, or he might become impatient, and "the Christian have to fight terribly hard to suppress and expel the pagan." Even when one was, as I tried to be, exactly on time, impatience sometimes made him irritable. He had been expectant for hours, or so he made one feel.

I always ran the last few yards to the high green gate at 5 Acacia Road in St. John's Wood, pushed it open, and stopped just inside to wait for Kot, framed in the kitchen window, to lift his head from a book and wave a welcome. And often I forgot to close the gate in my pleasure at having arrived.

There he was, as certain as spring, sitting in his kitchen, the stove blazing away at his back, the rows of plates shining on the dresser at his right, and a straight chair placed opposite him at the scrubbed deal table, waiting. This kitchen was a hearth in the most ancient sense of the word, and Kot regarded it as such. Not the slightest disorder was permitted. The extreme plainness of the furniture seemed a sanctity; the tomatoes in a bowl on the dresser, the loaf of bread, spoke of peace and joy, as alive as they might be if Cézanne had painted them:

> And whether He exists at all,
> The Father and the Prodigal,
> He is expected by these things
> And each plate Hosannah sings.

Kot's eyes, behind horn-rimmed glasses, snapped with eagerness; his wiry gray hair stood up two inches straight in the air like the *élan vital* itself. He looked astonished and fiercely expectant. When he laughed, his whole face broke up into laughter, and enjoyment seemed to shoot out of him in showers of sparks. In every way, and about everything he did—reading a manuscript, washing sheets, building a fire—he was the opposite of superficial; he did everything with his whole being, and this meant, of course, that he used up an immense amount of energy and emotion in just the ordinary business of living. The rituals upon which he insisted, the definite rhythm of each day, were no doubt necessary as a balance.

So every detail had been foreseen hours before a visit. There on the table lay his box of Russian cigarettes, two cups and saucers, a jar of jam, and a tin box of thin English biscuits. Kot smoked incessantly, drank tea, ate nothing, but insisted that enormous quantities of jam and biscuits be consumed by the guest. And if the tea itself followed a ritual, so did the conversation. When I saw him alone—and he preferred to see his friends alone—Kot always began, "Well, May . . ." leaving a silence in the air while he turned to light his cigarette from a long paper spill held to the coals in the stove-grate behind him. This was an invitation to tell all that had taken place in the last days, where you had been, whom you had seen, and above all to give a detailed account of all meals. Kot, ascetic himself, loved descriptions of food. This was a safe beginning. For almost everyone turned out to be beyond the pale. "There are pigs and people," one would be informed, "and so-and-so is and always has been a pig." Argument was useless. Kot's mind had been made up, it appeared, before you were born. Rarely, very rarely, he gave the accolade, "Yes, so-and-so is a real person." That was high praise, indeed. His literary judgments, too, were implacable. For he was one of the rare readers who look upon the writing of literature as sacred work, and the betrayal of it by shoddiness, impatience, or simple lack of talent, as an actual crime.

D. H. Lawrence called him "The Lion of Judah," or, when they were in a state of war, simply "Jehovah," but that was in the golden age before World War I, long before I knew him. Leonard Woolf said, "If you knew Kot well, you understood what a major Hebrew prophet must have been like. If Jeremiah had been born in a ghetto

village of the Ukraine in 1882, he would have been Kot."
He was a Jew in the proudest possible way, breathing fire
and brimstone against all Philistines and "blighters" as
he called politicians, publishers, bad writers, and any
Jew who did not come up to his high standards: "I am
myself again and curse the blighters," he would say, a
fierce joy in his intense black eyes. He was intransi-
geance personified, could say "no" with an absolute disregard of the amenities or his own self-interest. When a
mutual friend of his and the Lawrences telephoned him
after twenty years absence from England, and asked
whether she might come to call, Kot said simply, "No."
For in the interval she had written a book about Lawrence of which he disapproved; in vain she pleaded that
after all they were old friends, that she needed him. Kot
simply repeated "No." It was final. But if he said "yes,"
it was "yes" forever and ever, world without end.

So the acceptance of a writer by Kot was an act of
faith. Like any true believer he would then brook no
criticism of someone like Lawrence or Katharine Mansfield whom he had accepted, although during their lifetime, he had himself criticized, badgered and given no
quarter. He had, in fact, elected himself a despotic conscience for his writer friends, and the name "Jehovah"
had been given, no doubt, after considerable suffering.
One did not write to Kot as to other friends; one wrote to
one's conscience, and this becomes quite clear when I
look back, for instance, at the letters Katharine Mansfield did write to him, as in November of 1921: "I am
glad you criticized me. It is right that you should have
hated much in me. I was false in many things and *care-
less*—untrue in many ways. But I would like you to know

that I recognize this and for a long time I have been trying to 'squeeze the slave out of my soul.' "

There in Kot's kitchen where we sat and talked and
smoked and he scolded me about my "terrible impatience" in that spring of 1937, I came slowly to recognize
my inner direction; the aspirations, doubts, arrogances
and painful beginnings of self-knowledge began to so-
lidify into a sense of vocation. Kot had an unerring eye
for the fake, the false note, the "literary," and would
have none of it. But he had also an unerring eye for the
significant, for the lasting, for the hard core of truth.
His belief in me, tempered by a great deal of harsh criticism, and based on the very long view, seemed like rock
under my feet. I began to face then that it would take
me a great many years, the rest of my life, to become
what I might eventually become as a writer.

But many of our meetings were just pure joy, especially when James Stephens and I were invited together.
Then Kot prepared a Martini of his own invention (mysterious herbs were added to the usual ingredients). After
two or three helpings of this powerful drink, James
would shut his eyes and rock back and forth as he recited poems in that unforgettable crooning voice of his,
while Kot sat and beamed. Then, when we were all
three properly intoxicated, I might dare to read a new
poem for James's criticism; and finally Kot himself might
speak about Russia, the Russia of his youth, the Russia
of the Martinis. It was marvelous to hear him tell of
spring in Russia, how after the dark and terrible cold,
suddenly the air was full of the scent of violets and
people went literally mad with joy. The Russian in Kot
was never very deeply submerged. Just under the thin

[ *213* ]

English surface, the Russian suffered and rejoiced and led his natural passionate life. The crocuses in the garden reminded him of the candles in the synagogues. When he spoke the word "Kiev" (where he had studied as a young man) hundreds of churches seemed to rise up behind his eyes, suddenly very bright, and one heard the sound of bells. Kot was not orthodox, but like many "unbelievers" he was a deeply religious person, so much so that he felt it sacrilege to profane a church or a cathedral by entering it as a mere tourist. Only once he was persuaded by Lady Ottoline Morell to attend a service in St. George's chapel at Windsor, and on this occasion was amazed and delighted to discover that the service seemed very much like an orthodox Jewish one.

Sometimes the Russian Kot was startling: we heard fantastic tales about the neighbors next door, whom he always called "the mad ones." They were a Dostoevskian group, never very clearly defined, of whom one was definitely subhuman and the others given to fits of hysteria; Kot accepted them as part of his universe and related their antics with considerable zest. Number 5 Acacia Road is one half of a double house, and the walls were thin, so that any sound next door was audible—and the sounds were apt to be horrifying. "With the new year, the mad ones have taken a new lease of life, and are screaming day and night. This is a sign of warm weather arriving." In fact when at last 5 Acacia Road was empty again, and silent, there was a sense of absence, of something missing. As Kot expressed it, "At any time I prefer mad ones to sane, normal human beings." They, at least, were not "blighters."

Besides all these subjects of discourse when James

Stephens was there, there was always the entirely fantastic subject of money. Hopes rose and fell each year with the results of the Irish sweep. "If I win the Irish sweep, I shall be your publisher and there will be no need to deal with the blighters." But if all else failed, there was, floating in the magic bottle of Martinis, a scheme by which Kot, James and I would live at the zoo in a comfortable cage with all food and drink provided free. "If you and James are in a cage with me, I shall no longer need or want anything. And the end of my days will be passed in happiness, serene and complete." This dream collapsed, of course, when Julian Huxley left the London Zoo, for we could hardly accept a cage from a total stranger.

Just as when I was with him, I have been suspended in time during the writing of these pages about Kot, and it is hard to believe that he is dead. Yet, if there is a Heaven, it looks exactly like 5 Acacia Road. Kot is sitting at the kitchen table, pronouncing, "In the hierarchy of creation there is God Almighty and Leo Tolstoy"; Lawrence is putting a duck in the oven; K. M. is writing at her table in the upper room; James is drinking gin and crooning poems; and down at the end of the garden the pear tree is in flower.

The two springs of 1936 and 1937 melt into each other for me now; they are woven together into a single web of new friendships that were to nourish and sustain me through all the later years. They were a great burst of life. But I cannot leave them without going back for a moment to evoke the end of my stay at Taviton Street. Shortly before I was leaving for Belgium, John Summerson, as a farewell present, took me to dinner at Elizabeth Bowen's.

At precisely a quarter to eight on that warm May evening, we set out in a taxi for Clarence Terrace on Regent's Park. If I had imagined that a "Terrace" might turn out to be something like a "Mansion" or a "Garden" this was but another proof of my abysmal ignorance; John soon put me right, and showed me the beauty of the Nash designs, the great windows, the cream-colored façades with their balconies and pillars that look like a long elegant palace, and are really sets of houses. We drew up before one of these. Who was there? What happened that evening? I remember it as a daze of happiness, intensified by the poignance of departure. I remember vividly our entrance into the upstairs drawing room, its great French windows open onto the May night, so the heavy curtains seemed to breathe gently, and one was drawn irresistibly to look out, to look down onto the Park, the silent groves of trees lit up by the street lamps like stage scenery, and a patch of moonlight below shivering the lake. I remember turning back, to the bowl of white peonies on the mantel reflected in a Regency mirror above them, white peonies with a streak of crimson jagged at their centers; I remember Elizabeth Bowen herself, sitting on the immense stiff Regency sofa looking like a Holbein drawing, the fine red hair pulled back from her forehead, speaking in small rushes, and too observant (one guessed) to allow herself any but the most fleeting glances at a shy guest, so she was apt to stare fixedly at a cigarette in her hand; like the peonies on the mantel, she resembled a swan, stately, slightly awkward, beautiful and haunting. And I remember Alan

[ 216 ]

Cameron, her husband, though here again the images merge, for I grew only later to appreciate the acute sensitivity and kindness beneath his slightly Blimpish appearance, and his mask of pretended irascibility. We shared a devotion to all members of the cat family, and went sometimes to the zoo in later years, to look, in the grave and beautiful faces of leopards and lions and even tigers, for the portrait of Elizabeth. I think of a midnight years after that first meeting, when I watched Alan walk up and down that room, a glass in his hand, and recite the first page of *The Death of the Heart*, breaking off to shout in his rather high voice, "That's genius!" But on that first evening my attention was focused on the shy heron, John Summerson, talking with animation, at home in this world where I felt still so strange, and sending Elizabeth Bowen into a ripple of sustained laughter, like a musical accompaniment, something between a purr and a song.

That room must still reverberate with the voices of all the friends who gathered there, and all the "occasions," public and private, when love and wit and grace and passion were floating about in the air, magnetized by the presence of Elizabeth. It was there that I first met Virginia Woolf, and with the evoking of that vanished personification of genius, I shall close this chapter of joys, all undeserved, as the final flower in the bouquet I held in my hands. I had, one day, earlier in that spring of 1937, wrapped a copy of my first book of poems carefully in tissue paper, had stopped in Russell Square to ease its passage with the purchase of a bunch of primroses, and then had walked in fear and trembling to 52

Tavistock Square where Virgina and Leonard Woolf lived at that time.

The door was opened by a kindly old servant in an apron, who received the package, and asked whether I would not like to come up. But one does not batter one's way in to see the gods, and I hastily withdrew. A few days later I received a note in that delicate spidery hand to say that Virginia Woolf thanked me and had not yet had time to read the poems. I was disappointed, of course, for at that time, her word about the beginnings of my work seemed to me, in the intensity of my admiration, the only accolade which could possibly matter. I have since learned how overwhelming are the demands for the "attention" of a recognized author, but I did not know it then, and I felt dashed.

Then Elizabeth Bowen, to whom I had related this story, arranged a little dinner party, and I was formally introduced. Virginia Woolf came into the drawing room at Clarence Terrace, visibly shy, for an instant like a deer or some elegant wild creature dazzled by the lights, and walked straight across the room to stand in one of the long windows, looking out into the Park. She was, as has been sufficiently stated, far more beautiful than any of the photographs show, and perhaps less strange, and that night, in a long green *robe-de-style*, she looked exactly as one had imagined she would look. It was a moment of total recognition and delight. Later on that evening she realized that it was I who had left poems and primroses at her door, and the ice was finally broken. She told me how someone had just presented her with a small Chinese vase, and how improbable it seemed that at that very moment primroses should appear out of thin air, to be placed in it. I was invited to tea the next week.

This time I saw her alone, in the small upstairs drawing room which contained so many patterns and small bright objects it gave the impression of being like the inside of a kaleidoscope: a screen painted by Vanessa Bell, flowered prints on the chairs, a wall of French books in many-colored paper covers, and two hassocks by the fire upon one of which I sat, suffering a crisis of shyness. Virginia Woolf, like the elephant's child in Kipling, was a woman of "insatiable curtiosity," as well as rippling malice. She may have looked like some slightly unreal goddess, transparent to every current of air or wave, the eyes set in the sculptured bone in such a way that their beauty was perfectly defined; her conversation was anything but ethereal. I remember that we laughed hilariously, that she teased me about poetry, and told me that it was easy to write poems and immensely difficult to write novels. But when I stammered out that I was actually at work on a novel at the moment, she looked at me with sudden intensity, and said, "You are writing a novel? Ah, then all this must seem totally unreal to you." *The Years* had just been published; I did not think it the best of her novels, nor, I think, did she. For she spoke of it that day as an immense act of will, to break the mold of *The Waves;* she said that someone had called her on the telephone, a disembodied voice like that of a sybil, and had said, "You are becoming too special, too involved in your own inner world. Come back to us." So she labored at *The Years,* which was, she said, to be "about ordinary people." She had worked at it in a curious way, many scenes at a time, picking out first one and then another like the pieces of a mosaic. So that the horror in this case, as she explained, had been the transitions, the linking passages.

At precisely six Leonard Woolf appeared. I felt at once that his arrival was a signal: it was time for me to leave. I felt this, but I also felt that it would be rude to rush away, and, caught in the dilemma, found myself launching into a glowing description of Whipsnade, of the restaurant and the tigers among the hawthorns; suddenly before I knew it, I had invited the Woolfs to come out for dinner.

I have no illusions about this event: the charms that brought them driving thirty miles out of London were not mine, but the bait of a very good restaurant indeed, and my glowing description of the wonders of the place. Everything went wrong, of course. The sky was heavily overcast, great black clouds rising up over Whipsnade Hill. The Woolfs were late, so that the visit to the animals had to be curtailed, and because it was late, various delights I had held out failed to materialize. We did not see one wallaby with a baby in her pocket. The icy wind blew in our faces, and I feared that I might be responsible for giving one of England's glories an attack of pneumonia. It was a long walk to the tigers, but we did —from far off—hear a strange sad mewing. When we got to the round cages, a little like huge aviaries with trees, grass, hawthorn in flower inside them, there was nothing whatever to be seen, not a single tiger face, or even a paw, not a single round ear behind a bush. I was in a state of acute embarrassment and misery, which was not relieved when we discovered that the great cats had all been put to bed in boxlike cages to one side of their green paradise, and were complaining sadly. However, on the way back, we did have one redeeming pleasure, the sight of the baby giraffe, who had been born only a few weeks before, running gaily up and down his paddock, his short tail flying, and such a ridiculous gamboling air despite his long rocking-horse neck, that we laughed aloud, forgetting the black clouds and the icy wind. Was it then or later, that I saw that Virginia Woolf looked rather like a giraffe—her immense dark eyes, long aristocratic neck, and slightly disdainful, sensitive way of lifting her chin?

Fortunately the restaurant provided an excellent *Filet Mignon* with *sauce béarnaise;* we had a bottle of claret, and the deer did come and stare at us through the plate-glass windows. We had coffee upstairs in my rooms, so that Virginia Woolf could smoke one of her long thin elegant cigars. What did we talk about? I was too overwhelmed with responsibility to register, as depressed as a circus manager whose acts have all failed to perform. I felt I had persuaded them to a long journey only to find some poor miserable tigers mewing in their boxes: a fiasco.

Much later, during the Battle of Britain, I heard that the baby giraffe had died of fright in a bombing, that gay gambol turned into a hideous terrified gallop and failure of the heart. And shortly afterward, when I was in Chicago on a lecture trip, someone quite casually handed me a newspaper clipping. It contained a brief statement that Virginia Woolf early that morning had walked down to the River Ouse and drowned herself. I remember how, in an instant of acute grief and recognition, the two images slid together for me. After a long silence I wrote to Leonard Woolf. "I have very vivid recollection of that evening at Whipsnade," he answered, "which now seems to belong to another world and age. It was June 30, 1937."